Choosing the Perfect Dog for You and Your Family

Choosing the Perfect Dog for You and Your Family

Mordecai Siegal

CB
CONTEMPORARY
BOOKS
CHICAGO

Library of Congress Cataloging-in-Publication Data

Siegal, Mordecai.
    Choosing the perfect dog for you and your family /
Mordecai Siegal.
      p.   cm.
    Includes index.
    ISBN 0-8092-3709-1 (paper)
    1. Dogs.   2. Dogs—Selection.   3. Dog breeds.
4. Dogs—Training.   5. Dogs—Social aspects.
6. Children and animals.   I. Title.
SF426.S58   1994
636.7'0887—dc20   93-49466
                                                  CIP

Photographs by Creszentia Allen on pages 34, 37, 38, 40, 41, 43, 44, 46, 48, 49, 51, 52, 54, 56, 58, 59, 60, 63, 64, 65, 67, 69, 70, 72, 74, 76, 78, 80, 81, 83, 85, 86, 88, 89, 91, 93, 94, 95, 96, 98, 100, 101, 103, 105, and 109.

Photograph by Dan Farrell on page 126.

Photograph by Marion J. Levy, Jr., on page 114.

Photographs by Mordecai Siegal on pages viii, 3, 4, 7, 8, 10, 13, 14, 22, 106, 130, 139, 140, 146, 149, 154, 163, and 175.

Adapted from *A Dog for the Kids* © 1984 by Mordecai Siegal.

Copyright © 1994 by Mordecai Siegal
All rights reserved
Published by Contemporary Books, Inc.
Two Prudential Plaza, Chicago, Illinois 60601-6790
Manufactured in the United States of America
International Standard Book Number: 0-8092-3709-1
10   9   8   7   6   5   4   3   2   1

To *my* family—
Vicki, TJ, Ida, and Jasper—
with love and appreciation

CONTENTS

——1——
WHAT DOGS MEAN
TO CHILDREN

Most dogs are initially purchased for the benefit of children. Parents aren't really sure why they do this, other than it seems to be a good idea. Puppies are sweet-looking and adorable and give the unsuspecting parent the notion that they make wonderful toys. The truth is they are nothing at all like toys. Puppies quickly become grown dogs, certainly a lot sooner than children become adults. A grown dog bears little resemblance in appearance or behavior to the puppy it once was. When a new puppy first arrives, the excitement is overwhelming and clouds all reality . . . for a short while.

There is a new dog in the house. It's cheaper than a season in Europe, a house on the beach, or even summer camp. The family would rather have a doggy than any of those things.

"A dog of my own. Oh boy."

It's baby powder, Sesame Street, and training wheels all rolled into one delicious pie. The magic moment of arrival

1

is a giggly, near-hysterical time for kids, canines, and innocent bystanders. The dog somehow knows he has ended his perplexing journey and found a home. His new family looks way down at him on the floor, scoops him up, and cuddles him like a newborn. The froth, however, begins to settle with the first yelp of the dog and cry of the child. A tail was pulled and a finger nipped. The dog poops on the carpet and the little mistress and master step in it. There is a howl and a holler as parents, pup, and pupils run for the hills. How do you handle a hungry dog with nasty coming from both ends?

A turning point has been reached in the relationship between family and pooch and it's only the first hour of arrival. Unless the family knows what it is doing, things are going to get worse. There is probably nothing quite as miserable as the first seven nights with a newly adopted puppy or young dog. If you don't know what to do, you are probably ready to forgo the animal's innocence and quietly strangle it. But, alas, the children are watching. The new member of the family must be treated with kid gloves. Getting the dog and the family to hit it off on a permanent basis, much less learning to live with dog behavior, requires some understanding of dogs, of families, and of dogs and families together.

In view of all this, one must ask, why get a dog at all? The answer is easy. The canine connection could easily become the most valuable experience your child will ever have short of school and four years with an orthodontist. There are two uniquely valuable aspects to getting a dog for the family. First, there is the value to the parents, and second, the value to the child.

If you ask any child why she or he wants a dog, the answer will have something to do with fun. For kids, dogs are stimulating and make great playmates. They do play well together and if you visit a good nursery school or kindergarten you will quickly discover that play is the principal activity. However, if you look closely you will also discover that the play is carefully orchestrated. Although there are periods of "free play," most of the time is spent in playlike learning activities. The reason for this is that professional teachers and child experts understand that play is

a learning experience. It is a reenactment of what is learned through the process of repetition, emulation, and, of course, instruction. Dogs are great teachers.

But this new member of the family means more than play to a child. Everyone needs a friend who will remain constant and loyal without qualifying the relationship. This kind of friend will not exact a price in exchange for solace and comfort. In day-to-day living there are many troubled times, often because of transitional periods of growth and development. There is a period of disequilibrium for every child prior to the achievement of new accomplishments, from learning to walk or speak to accepting a maturing body. Each new phase brings with it fear of the new way of being and a refusal to give up the old way. Trading off the security of dependency for the unknown factors of independence creates stormy emotions and a deeply felt ambivalence. When an infant crawls into a room, leaving the family behind in another, it is a significant first step to separating from mother and father and going off into the frightening world of adulthood. Do you remember how many times your child came crawling back from an empty room to the safety and comfort of your presence?

A normal dog responds sympathetically and most lovingly to the somber moods of children by providing quiet companionship or lively enticements to play or at least relate. It is a lucky child who has a pet during those times when life is difficult and the world does not seem to be a pleasant place. When a child is confused and troubled, her four-legged friend will always be there to offer a bit of warmth and friendship, consistency and unquestioned loyalty, and an unflagging desire to catch her eyes. Dogs are better than chicken soup. The love of a dog will ease the pains of growth. It gives a child a very real sense of security and identity, enabling the youngster to take some large risks and enter the next phase of growth and development. The dog is always there for the sad, happy, eager, or anxious kid.

From the parents' view, dogs provide the opportunity for emotional and psychological growth. To use an old-fashioned term that is often forgotten, dogs help children develop character. The way a child learns to handle and care for an animal helps in developing a healthy self-image. When children like themselves they believe they are worthwhile people. When children do not have a sound and healthy self-image, if they do not like themselves or if they believe others do not like them, they tend to show it by being aggressive or withdrawn. They may hurt others in order to ease their own inner pain. They may also withdraw into a shell, a personal private world, to protect themselves from what they believe is rejection. Obviously, the primary source of self-esteem in the very young comes from parents and then peers. But do not discount the influence of living with a dog.

Of all the benefits that children derive from their pets, including an understanding of birth, death, growth, and relationships, one of the most worthwhile gifts is a lesson in leadership. I don't mean leadership in the sense of high school graduation speeches or militaristic virtues but rather in the vital areas of independence, self-sufficiency, and competent self-management. If leadership is understood as the willingness to assume responsibility, to make decisions, to risk failure, then a child living with a pet is, indeed, involved with leadership. Dogs are capable of bringing out the best in a child or helping parents create values that are more learned than inherited. Parents become partners with the family dog and influence the development of self-control and inner focus in their children. These developments are not accomplished with mirrors or by regarding the dog as an assistant teacher. One does nothing unusual with the dog other than giving it normal care and attention. But parents must teach their children to regard the pet as a playmate, friend, and dependent member of the family. Thus, the child will assume a sense of responsibility for the dog's care, with the motivating factor being the reward of play and companionship.

By helping a child set realistic goals in regard to caring for the family dog, the child is more apt to experience the elated feelings associated with achievement and success. Success in caring for a dog in turn allows children to feel competent in dealing with life's problems as they are encountered. All children can help in some degree with feeding, walking, grooming, training, and loving the dog. Even some medical problems can be handled by *everyone* in the family.

Allow your kids to shop for the dog's needs and participate in the decision-making processes associated with food selection, toys, bedding, and training. It is quite reassuring for the child to discover that she has an important role in her family because they care about how she feels and what she thinks, says, and does. It is rewarding to encourage the kids to express their thoughts, feelings, and ideas concerning the dog. Discussions about the dog's welfare are not

only useful but give the entire family an opportunity to relate to one another about something meaningful.

The initial decision to acquire a dog for the family may have been based on an impulse, a desire to give your children yet one more plaything, or because of someone else's influence. Although these are not really the best of reasons, still, the initial decision was a good one, with your heart in the right place. For whatever reason you decided to get a dog, it was a fortunate, valid idea. Parents are the unsung heroes of dog ownership. They deserve awards and medals for leading the way to happy pet relationships. When a child begs for a puppy, and most do, it is Mom and Dad who really accept the brunt of the work and do so because they know it brings pleasure and happiness. They recognize the special place dogs have in American family life.

THE FAMILY WAY

What Dogs Can Mean to Different Children

The typical family. It is probably not possible to define the typical family, but for the purpose of exploring various situations in which dogs live I will try. Here I refer to a group in which one or more children live with both parents. There are no unusual situations demanding more of the dog or the family other than typical day-to-day activities and problems. To the kids in this situation, a dog is a sort of brother or sister without all the bickering and competition for attention.

The dog becomes a pal and a teacher at the same time. It's no secret that children are intensely interested in animals and all things pertaining to animals. This interest offers parents the unique opportunity to stimulate learning in their children and, at the same time, wield significant influence over the development of character traits based on important moral codes of behavior. Learning to relate to a dog automatically involves a child's ability and desire to be fair-minded and humane.

Studies have revealed that in families across America the most popular member of the household is the pet. Most people regard their dogs as full-fledged members of the family. The reasons given are that dogs and other pets are responsive to the family's feelings and anxieties. Many pet owners stated that their pets are sensitive to family illness, depression, anger, tension, turmoil, happiness, and excitement. New friendships and social contact result because of the animal's presence in the house. There is even evidence of greater family harmony along with more hours spent together. Many of the pet owners who were surveyed noted that they like to think of their furry friends as being nearly human because of their feelings and contributions to the quality of family life.

In a typical family situation the dog can mean a great deal to the kids, but primarily as a dog. In other words, a pet is a superb companion and playmate that also requires children to demonstrate kindness and some sense of responsibility. As a member of the typical family, the dog is highly valued but at the same time related to without intensity or unusual need.

The divorced family. There is no possibility for a dog, new or otherwise, to play the role of a missing parent. Most people have been exposed to those who foolishly, or sensibly, use an animal as a substitute human. But in the case of children trying to cope with a broken family, the use of a dog as a substitute parent is not only foolhardy but risks psychological damage. People cannot be replaced. Children should not be asked to feel better about something when they do not. Adult responses asked (or demanded) of a child tend to retard the child's emotional growth. Trying to

fill a void with a dog when that void is caused by the loss of a person courts emotional retreat and a feeling of failure. These feelings are heaped upon all the other bad feelings brought about by family change.

A child's mother or father or even a dog, for that matter, can never be replaced if you believe that we are all one of a kind. The relationship between a mother and a father represents the primary relationship in the lives of children.

Parents are the role models for kids, the source of safety, security, and what's real and what isn't. A dog can never fill that bill. However, dogs can be quite important to children in other ways during the crisis presented by a changed family.

The most common negative feelings in children during and after a divorce have to do with guilt, a sense of loss, and, most destructive of all, the loss of self-esteem. Children tend to believe that they, somehow, have caused their parents to separate. This feeling, plus the sense of failure sometimes brought on by comparison to families that have not split up, helps to create a very poor self-image. A dog can help a child improve his self-image.

Feeling good about oneself is the primary benefit to a child, or anyone else for that matter, who lives with a dog. Learning to handle and care for a dog competently helps people to develop a positive self-image. That sense of self also comes from the feeling of being loved and needed by the animal. The consistency of a dog's affection, his needs, his unqualified acceptance of human caretakers, will break through all emotional barriers in children and with one slurp across the face make a child feel better. After all, if a child is certain of being loved and needed, how can he feel bad about himself? How can he have doubts about his worth? A dog can make him happy, and happiness is an ongoing feeling that can grow from within and stay with the child for a lifetime.

Single-parent family. The problems that arise when one parent leaves home because of divorce or when a parent dies are complicated and difficult. Here the role of the dog is to help the child feel competent and worthwhile. But in the case of the single-parent home in which the mother or father has chosen a lifestyle of single parenthood from the very beginning, the dog's place can be unique. As previously stated, a dog who is a member of a single-parent family probably adds much to the child's feeling of having what other children have. While not actually a substitute parent, the dog becomes an integral part of the family. The level of status and importance accorded to such a family dog approaches that of brother or sister, with the dog rewarded with greater standing and privilege than the average pet. In fact, I can think of no family situation where the dog is more valuable than in the single-parent arrangement.

The parent must make every effort to make having a dog a success. These efforts will be challenged by the hours devoted to a job, day care or baby-sitter service, and the exhaustion felt at the end of often completely filled days. It will be difficult, indeed, caring for the dog's needs, especially a young dog in need of housebreaking and obedience training. The reward will be in the comfort and security provided to the child by the dog. As the family pet becomes an important factor in the child's life, it represents a fleshing out of the family structure along with a constant, reliable source of added love and comfort. A devoted dog, one who has been trained to behave himself, takes up a great deal of the emotional slack for the child whose needs can drain one human being. Single parents help their children and themselves when they take on the chore of living with a dog. All the bother associated with the first months with a puppy is worthwhile. The canine family addition is as essential as burgers, shakes, friends, and a glass with a cartoon on it, too.

Families with physically or emotionally disabled kids.
The need for parental love and guidance notwithstanding, the greatest gifts given to disabled children are self-esteem, pride, and as much independence as possible. A dog can

help such a child, at least in part. Family and community support are the most important elements of success, but having a dog can provide a positive impact as well.

The most useful role the dog plays for the disabled child is that of a faithful and loyal friend. Dogs have no prejudice toward other dogs or people. Race, religion, sexual orientation, or physical and mental capacities play no role in the giving or withholding of affection or approval. Once a person makes the effort to relate to and take charge of a dog, the two creatures connect for life. It is one of nature's gifts. Even seriously disabled children can do something involving a dog's needs. The giving of affection or approval is not taken lightly by the dog and is received with more than a little gratitude. The stroke of a brush or the filling of a food bowl are not difficult tasks but mean a great deal to the dog, who will regard the provider as a benevolent master or mistress. When a pet comes to a disabled child in need of something and that child is able to fulfill the need, the dog has done his job well.

Rich families, poor families, large families, and small families. The benefits of having a dog are a common denominator of all families large or small, rich or poor. Both rich and poor kids learn the same lesson from living with and caring for a dog. A coyote-looking mutt or a Cavalier King Charles Spaniel both must take to the street

to pursue the demands of digestion. The kids in charge of humble or grand dogs must still clean the doggy-do from the streets in order to comply with laws of most cities. Caring for dogs requires work, effort, and intelligence. These are the same requirements for managing money or learning to acquire it.

To an only child, a dog is both a friend and a relative who offers companionship while demanding the same sort of sharing as would a brother or sister. An only child will learn to respect the needs and feelings of others by satisfying the demands made by a dog. If the child withholds such respect, the dog will not provide the child with satisfaction. If you don't play ball, your dog won't roll over.

Conversely, a dog living in a family with many children offers an opportunity for some exclusive attention to be paid to the child that works for it. A dog cannot relate to the entire clan at once, at least not all the time. For the caring, giving child in a large family, the dog will extend itself with something extra, almost with gratitude. Here the pet is really the family dog in the fullest sense of the word, and it offers the parents and their children a unique opportunity for shared responsibility. The entire family will need to participate in a serious discussion in order to work out who does what for the dog. Schedules and work charts are useful and a spirit of cooperation is absolutely necessary. Taking care of the dog should be a family project that draws everyone together. Each member of the family will benefit in some way from the experience.

Childhood begins with a wet slap while hanging upside down. A half-forgotten dream, it is the beginning of the gradual process of becoming a full-fledged human being. Children, the youngest members of the family, are delicate saplings, vulnerable but overflowing with joyful promise.

They are beautiful. They are also valuable. The worth of the world can be found in the innocent vision of children. They are the gift of renewal and our only hope. Somewhere between the first breath of infancy and the last complaint of adolescence, adoring parents must step back and let them go. But before that uncertain step is taken, one should assess the quality of a childhood inevitably spent in delight, wonder, agony, and human fruition. Success and failure are relative terms, one not necessarily canceling the other. Keeping score is without value, but acceptance of our young as they are while continuing support and encouragement is priceless. Holding two little arms as two little legs wobble their first step is significant. Wiping tears and tickling bellies and explaining the rain are also significant. Childhood is a measurement of time during which one grows to full height and humanity. It is not complete without the reflection of ourselves in nature. Children and dogs complete the equation. Children are important and so are the dogs who share their lives.

It is quite clear that children and dogs have an undeniable need for each other. Those who spend the better part of childhood together with a dog will have something more valuable than money in the bank or straight-A report cards. The free expression of emotion, the desire to live with others, and the ability to accept responsibilities are part of entering the adult world. Children learn much of this from dogs they have known and loved. What a bunch of lucky dogs!

—2—
WHICH DOG?

If you ask a child to pick a dog, he may point and say, "I want the big orange one," and you and the family get stuck with a furry cow that's bigger than your kitchen. Don't do it. Be brave and tell the family to do its homework when the subject of choosing a dog comes up. I advise you to leave the final decision to the grownups. If you aren't happy with the new family dog, then sooner than you can say "scoop law" everyone is going to be miserable. Trust me.

Acquiring a dog is as easy as having a baby. If you stay in one spot long enough something will happen. Try to make a decision out of the event. Stay away from the pet shop windows full of huggable puppies with their noses smack up against the glass, begging for you, just you alone. Watch out for sad stray dogs, neighbors bearing gifts, rescued dogs, abandoned dogs, and dogs that follow your children home. For those who feel the pressure rising from the family ranks with subtle hints around the breakfast table like, "Please pass the dogberries," or "My cereal says snap, crackle, and *pup*," look them in the eye and respond with something official like, "Thank you for your suggestions. They are being considered by the management!" The best thing is to do nothing until you have given the matter some intelligent thought.

Unfortunately, most people enter the world of pet ownership through a series of chance circumstances and uncontrolled impulses. More puppies are purchased each year as a last-minute Christmas gift than at any other time. Dogs that are gifts are like in-laws who come to live with you shortly after being introduced. It is like being trapped at a potluck supper. Do not obey those very human responses to the chance dog. Acquisitions of this sort can be correctly classified as accidents. Obviously, many happy pet situations can result from the aforementioned possibilities, but the risk of disenchantment is quite high.

When human beings are dissatisfied with a pet dog, it means the animal doesn't fit in with their lifestyle. The apartment or house was too small, the animal was too big, too wild, not wild enough. In any case, the animal's future, indeed its very life, is in jeopardy. When getting divorced from a pet, the choices are limited and not very pleasant. One may find it another home (not too easy to accomplish), place the dog in a shelter (where it will probably be put to sleep), or abandon it (which is immoral for the human and deadly for the dog). It is very hard on children to face giving up a dog, even if it bit someone or destroyed fifteen thousand dollars' worth of furniture. It can be a wrenching emotional experience, one you'll not forget so easily. The best way to avoid such a situation is to be certain you get a dog that is well suited to your lifestyle.

The most common reason to acquire a dog is companionship, and that's about the best reason there is. Of course there are also dogs who work for a living, although they are very rarely kept primarily as pets. There are also many owners who maintain show dogs and campaign them for both pleasure and sport. This legitimate activity is enjoyed by many of the most humane and knowledgeable dog lovers in the country. There is also a place for children in the world of show dogs. The American Kennel Club (AKC) sanctions Junior Showmanship competitions at AKC all-breed or specialty shows. Here, kids between ten and seventeen years of age are judged in the ring on their ability and skills as show-dog handlers. Ribbons, prizes, and awards are given to the winners. For more information, contact the American Kennel Club, 51 Madison Avenue, New York, New York, 10010. An alternative to the AKC is the United Kennel Club, Inc. (UKC), which is the world's second largest all-breed purebred dog registry. More than 60 percent of its 6,600 annually licensed activities are working dog events. UKC activities include conformation dog shows, obedience trials, and hunting retriever tests. The AKC awards Champion titles for qualifying dogs. UKC additionally awards Grand Champion titles to qualifying dogs. Although there are important differences between the two organizations, they both perform similar functions for those involved in the dog sport. For more information, contact the United Kennel Club, 100 East Kilgore Road, Kalamazoo, Michigan, 49001.

Of late, some people have acquired dogs for protection only to find that they have exchanged one danger for another. Without consummate professionalism, protection dogs can be lethal, especially to children who innocently come in contact with them. It is essential before acquiring a dog that you ask yourself why you want it, how will it function in your life, and if that reason is conducive to fifteen years of pet ownership. Nothing less will do.

WHERE TO GET A DOG

Adoption agencies. For economic or humane considerations, there is no better place to obtain a dog or a puppy than your local animal shelter. Most cities and towns maintain a dog pound, SPCA-type organization, or animal adoption agency. These places can be found by looking in the yellow pages under Animal Shelters. Adopting a dog from an agency is a good deal for the animal as well as for the human. You will most likely be saving the dog from euthanasia. The pet will cost far less than in any commercial situation. Using an adoption agency is possibly the least expensive way to purchase a dog.

Most agencies today require that the animal be neutered so that it will not be able to add to the enormous population of homeless pets. Some shelters perform the service for reduced rates or no fee at all. Do not be surprised if you are asked to sign a contract agreeing to have the animal spayed (for a female) or castrated (for a male) within a set period of time. There are many good reasons to comply. It is not only humane but also healthy for the dog and very convenient for the dog's new family. Neutered females are less susceptible to mammary tumors. Neutered males are usually less aggressive and least likely to fight other dogs.

Breeders. Noncommercial and serious amateur breeders are the ideal sources for the best of the purebred dogs. These sources are especially important if you are at all interested in the showring and the high price of the dog is not too serious a problem. The noncommercial breeder is in the process of developing a line of dogs that will enhance his or her reputation and sense of fulfillment. He or she strives for breed perfection through an understanding of genetics and *socializing* techniques. (To socialize a puppy is to develop its adaptability to humans and to maximize its potential as a domestic house pet and companion.) Such breeders are, as a group, knowledgeable about selecting good dogs for mating and are in constant touch with other serious breeders. This type of breeder is usually interested in "breaking even" financially with not much thought of profit, or at least large profit. Noncommercial breeders enjoy the demands of breeding and developing winning dogs that eventually become champions of record with the American Kennel Club or the United Kennel Club. With few exceptions, they are ethical and quite selective about whom they sell one of their pups to.

Many commercial breeders are just as knowledgeable and ethical as noncommercial breeders. Although they are involved with breeding as a business, commercial breeders usually maintain high standards. However, it is difficult for those who are unacquainted with the world of dog breeding to sort out who is producing sound, healthy dogs on a selective basis and who is not. I am a bit more than cautious when a storefront operation selling puppies and young dogs sports blue ribbons and mounted plaques indicating champion dogs. These displays often represent a style of exploitation that is obviously being used as a sales tool and not necessarily indicative of high-quality dogs. Many breeds have been overpopularized and subsequently ruined by mass breeding while at the same time the breeder utilizes a few winning dogs for display and sales purposes. Before you buy a dog, find out about the seller and his stock. Ask around. Do not be afraid of blunt questions about any dog's parents and progenitors and get the answers in writing if you can.

Pet shops. A handful of pet shops breed their own dogs while a few others obtain their animals from decent, local commercial breeders. These often produce sound dogs of "pet quality," which simply means the dogs are not absolutely perfect representations of their breed. However, because of the laws of supply and demand, most pet shops must obtain their "live stock" from sources that can supply the quantity needed for a large business. This is where the trouble starts for the typical dog owner.

A large number of puppies sold in many pet shops come from so-called puppy mill operations that are scattered

throughout the midwestern and eastern parts of the United States. Arkansas, Kentucky, Iowa, Nebraska, Kansas, Missouri, and Illinois (and a few other states such as Pennsylvania and Ohio) are the main sources of puppies bred under the most dreadful, inhumane, and unhealthy conditions imaginable. A puppy mill is usually a small farm that maintains a cramped, dirty kennel area jammed with male and female dogs that are constantly mating, gestating, and whelping puppies in large quantities. There is no genetic consideration, no culling out of animals that are either unhealthy or from unhealthy parents. Certainly, dogs that are hyperactive, vicious, nervous, or overly shy are not taken out of the breeding program. The same is true of dogs possessing illnesses. Eye diseases, hip disorders, and all manner of ailments are ignored in such operations. Everything that breathes is mated, and mated too frequently, as if on an assembly line. Time is money. Indiscriminate breeding is money.

Ironically, many a good dog has been purchased from a pet shop and there are always enough exceptions to the rule to give one doubt. But there is no way for an inexperienced dog owner to know for sure what he or she is getting into. Many dog diseases such as hip dysplasia, progressive retinal atrophy, and congenital heart defects do not show up until the dog is somewhat grown. There are many, many illnesses and defects that are simply passed from one generation of puppy mill dogs to another. However, in all fairness, the same problems are known to afflict reputable breeders' stock. The principal difference is that breeders are more likely to make good on a defective dog and in most instances they will make efforts to eradicate the defect from their line of dogs. The fact is, however, that the large majority of dogs in the United States are purchased from pet shops.

HOW TO SELECT A DOG

There is no such thing as an ugly puppy. They are all appealing and lovable and many of us want to take them all home on first sight. With their large, pleading eyes and impish stances they creep right into your heart and make it very difficult to choose one from among the many available. But you must maintain your cool so that you do not purchase the first fur ball that licks your finger and yelps for your attention: he may have ringworm, be a potential fear biter, and suffer from deafness all in one package. How would you know if the seller didn't tell you? You must make some effort to discriminate between puppies that are physically and mentally sound and those that are not.

It is impossible to predict how an eight- to twelve-week-old puppy is going to turn out, but the dog's pedigree will tell you something. If there are several champions in the dog's genealogy, you are on the right track. If possible, examine the pup's dam or sire. One or the other (sometimes both) should be available for inspection if you are dealing with a breeder. Assuming you have done your homework and familiarized yourself with the standards of the breed, you can tell to some degree if the dog in question is half-good. Because most breeders take great pride in their dog's bloodlines, they try to steer you to a good specimen. Most of you will be purchasing a dog as a pet rather than for the showring and you will be shown a "pet quality" dog. Do not be put off by the term or be upset because the breeder will not sell you a show dog. Breeders are only interested in having the best examples of their breed campaigned for a champion title in the showring. Pet quality dogs are almost always perfectly healthy dogs with sound temperaments. Quite often only one slight flaw makes the difference. Perhaps one hind leg turns out just a bit, the nose color is slightly off, or some other "flaw" that would disqualify the dog for the ring is present. Pet quality dogs are, for the most part, the best dogs in the world.

Beware of overly shy, timid, or aggressive puppies. What is heartwarming or cute at twelve weeks can be quite destructive at six or eight months of age. *Do not buy the puppy but the dog he will grow into.* Look for an outgoing, friendly dog who comes right up to you and does not hide in the corner or run in terror.

A healthy puppy has clear, bright eyes. The teeth should be almost white and the gums pink. Sometimes there is a natural black-spotted pigmentation on the gums. This is normal. There should be no liquid or crusty discharge from the animal's eyes, ears, or nose. Its coat must be loose, supple, and low lustered, with no bare patches. If there is one puppy that is obviously in bad health, either in the pet shop or in a breeder's kennel, do not pick any dog from that group. Pass them by.

Look for unnatural markings or discoloration in the eyes. A puppy with a distended belly may have internal parasites or some other ailment. If the dog has just been fed, the belly will be distended from that, too. Thus, you should try to view the pup two hours after feeding time. Do not pick a dog that is fat, thin, or unusually different from the rest of the litter. Watch for continual rubbing of the eyes, ears, or nose. These actions could be signs of skin disease, external parasites (mites), or infection. Some puppies are born deaf. Test for deafness by gently clapping your hands behind the dog and watch for a response. Do not purchase a puppy that is suffering from diarrhea or bloody stools.

With the breeder's permission, hold the puppy in your arms with the belly facing up. If the dog submits with ease and pleasure, his temperament is just fine. If he squirms desperately to get away, he may be aggressive or nervous. If he whines or whimpers, he may be shy or timid. These reactions are important for you to know. Place the dog on the ground and lie him on his back, holding him in position. If he struggles furiously with growls and snarls he has a very aggressive temperament and should not be brought into your home. Most families are best matched up with a dog of sound, even temperament. Do not pass up a dog with a passive or retiring temperament if you or your child happens to be quiet or shy. You may even wish to select a dog with a temperament that is different from yours or your family's. Some quiet, gentle adults or children do best with an outgoing dog. In essence, the temperament of the dog you choose represents a highly personal decision for you and your family. In the end, there is probably the right person or family for almost every dog.

Having selected a puppy, get a written record of the dog's inoculations that indicates dates, amounts, and types. Find out if the animal has just been wormed and any other medical history. This information will help your veterinarian. Ask for a written guarantee that the puppy can be returned if, after a veterinary examination, he is found to be poor in health. Do not leave without official papers from the American Kennel Club if the dog is represented as having been registered by the AKC. In most cases the litter has been registered and you will be given a form to mail to the AKC along with a registration fee.

Before making a final decision about selecting a breed of dog, you would be well advised to attend as many local dog shows as possible. As a matter of fact, attending local dog shows is a good idea even if you know what you want. A *benched* show is the best kind for this purpose because the dogs must remain in portable kennels (dog crates) until the judging is completed. At a benched show you can tour the benching area and closely examine the dogs and talk to their owners who are either noncommercial or amateur breeders. Unfortunately, not all shows are benched. Even at an *unbenched* show you can see many quality dogs and their breeders. More than likely you will make contact with a quality source for the dog of your dreams. If not, you can look for breeders' classified advertisements in magazines such as *Dog World, Dog Fancy, Pure-Bred Dogs,* or *American Kennel Gazette* (published by the AKC). Check the classified ads in your local newspaper as well. If all else fails, write to the American Kennel Club, 51 Madison Avenue, New York, New York, 10010, for a list of national breed clubs, each one of which can give you a list of breeders handling the kind of dog in which you are interested. One last word about selecting a dog. There is probably no one who deals with all the breeds in every conceivable living situation other than the professional dog trainer. Dog trainers can give you a truly objective opinion about any breed of dog as a pet or worker. Seek out an experienced, reputable dog trainer and go to him or her for topflight advice.

WHICH BREED FOR YOUR KIDS?

Of all the questions concerning dog ownership, I can think of none more important than which breed to choose. That initial decision is without a doubt the most important one. The second most important decision is selecting a dog with a good temperament. Temperament is more important than looks, intelligence, or cost. It is better to have a good-natured mutt with a scruffy multicolored coat than a manicured Toy Poodle who will open your veins when you go near his food bowl. If you are in the process of selecting a dog for your children, you owe it to yourself and your family, and to the dog as well, to go about the process with some degree of knowledgeability. Common sense will not necessarily help you.

Apart from aesthetics, selecting a specific breed of dog has more to do with how it fits in with your living conditions and your family situation. Some dogs have a hard time in a cramped apartment because they are quite active. There are breeds that are large, vigorous hunters with an incredible ability to run and yet they become quite inactive indoors. That would describe some surprisingly large breeds. Certain large breeds present an interesting set of qualities that make them ideal for some home situations. What seems more logical than getting a toy breed of dog for a young child? Unfortunately, it is not necessarily the best thing to do. Many toy breeds are not suitable for children. Despite the fact that toy breeds are among the finest of all dogs, the very qualities that make them so desirable to adults are exactly what make them unsuitable for many children. These demanding little creatures like to think of themselves as the blessed event of the family and become quite competitive with, if not downright intolerant of, children. Several toy breeds are openly hostile toward children while others are just too fragile for rough-and-tumble play. Pomeranians, as a rule, do not like children. A Yorkshire Terrier can break a bone just by falling off the bed. Despite a few exceptions, however, children and various toy breeds often have no problems hitting it off. In particular, older, gentler children or those who are more introspective often develop lifetime relationships with small dogs.

The American Kennel Club recognizes 136 dog breeds. These breeds are separated into seven *Groups* plus the *Miscellaneous Class* for breeds close to AKC recognition. Officially, most (but not all) of the very small breeds are part of the Toy Group. The eighteen breeds within this category range in height between six and twelve inches from the shoulder and between one and fourteen pounds, depending on the breed and selectivity of the breeder. The smallest of these dogs are referred to as "teacups." An older, considerate child can live with and care for any one of the dogs within the Toy Group. But the younger and/or less mature child should not be saddled with a dog he can accidentally harm or with a dog who might not want to share the spotlight of childhood.

The same caution should be used in selecting a terrier, especially the smaller breeds. West Highland White Terriers are adorable, loving family dogs, but they do not necessarily want to be the exclusive companion of a child. Airedales are larger, more protective but somewhat stubborn animals with both lovable and unlovable traits. Pugs are among the toy breeds that love and adore children. The rugged Pug makes an excellent playmate, except in the summer heat. Poodles are extremely intelligent, come in three varieties (Toy, Miniature, and Standard), and shed the least of all breeds. The Miniature Poodle and the Standard Poodle are the most suitable for children. English Springer Spaniels are among the best dogs for children. These dogs relate well to children and have an easygoing temperament. Fox Terriers are superstars. They are probably the most charming of all. These outgoing dogs are adept at tricks and try anything to get your attention. However, they are highly sensitive and excitable and unbelievably active indoors. They are capable of driving your family quite mad with their energy, barking, and demand for attention. They are also quite scrappy with other dogs. As you can see, each dog breed has a little something different to offer the first-time dog owner.

When you select a dog breed, try to find out what

exactly that breed was used for in its traditional role. For example, most people are not aware that the Poodle is essentially a retriever and one of the finest swimmers in the canine kingdom. The name *Poodle* comes from the German word *pudeln*, meaning "to splash in the water." In France it is called *Caniche*, from the French word *canard*, meaning "duck." The Poodle is a vigorous water dog that was originally used to assist duck hunters. This fact tells you that a Poodle has all the marvelous qualities of a retriever and needs exercise and mental stimulation as well. An occasional swim is a blessing for these dogs. If you read about the qualities of retrievers, you will be in a position to judge whether the Poodle suits your family needs.

It would be a mistake to believe that one breed or mixture is smarter, cleaner, or more lovable than another. An animal from well-bred stock with proper care and training is more likely to be the ideal pet than any other. The correct approach for choosing a dog is not which dog is best, but which dog best suits you. Do you like a huggy-kissy pet or one with an aloof sense of self? Large or small animal? Long-coated or short, and do you have the desire to fuss with a coat requiring daily grooming? Do not begin to shop for a dog until you've answered these basic questions. How much time, for instance, can you devote to grooming, exercising, or play? Various breeds require more or less attention with regard to these matters. Are your kids very young or are they around ten years of age? Do you want a male or female dog? There are many aspects to each sex that must be taken into account so that a sound choice can be made. Stud fees for males and valuable litters from females are not realistic considerations for the average pet owner with no knowledge of or facilities for breeding. There is no profit to be gained from dog breeding if you are an inexperienced amateur; therefore, it should not be a factor in selecting a male or a female.

Male dogs are larger animals and normally eat more food than females of the same breed. Males are somewhat more independent and are usually more difficult to obedience train. At the very least they require more handling. The male of the species is more likely to wander away (sometimes permanently) than the female and certainly he gets into more fights with other dogs. Many people admire these qualities and find themselves more attracted to male dogs. Some people find the machismo of a large male can be quite appealing.

Female dogs go into *heat* twice a year. Also called *estrus*, each period lasts approximately three weeks. During this time the animal secretes an odorous fluid in order to attract male dogs for the purpose of mating. When no puppies are desired the female dog must be kept away from male dogs, and that means being locked indoors. Many dog owners consider this a nuisance, while others consider it a small inconvenience in exchange for a gentle, easy-to-manage animal that at times needs to stay home.

The stereotypical attributes of males and females can be missing or distorted in an individual dog by poor breeding or early environmental influences such as gunshots, car backfires, or physical abuse. A viable option for solving some of the less desirable male or female traits is to spay the female (*ovariohysterectomy*) or castrate the male, assuming you have no intention of showing or mating the animal. These very common procedures are highly recommended. They enhance the animal's adaptability to family life and eliminate the possibility of unwanted puppies.

45 BREEDS THAT LOVE CHILDREN

To help parents select a dog for their children, a gallery of forty-five breeds is offered on the following pages. These breeds are accepted by many dog experts to be good with children. That means these dogs actually like kids and enjoy their company. It does not account for individual dogs within these breeds that may not hold true to their predictable breed traits. As mentioned before, mass breeding operations have produced millions of puppies that do not maintain original breed characteristics. Most of these pups show up in pet shops. However, both commercial and noncommercial breeders have managed to make negative contributions. Your only protection is to buy from a reputable source, get some form of guarantee, examine the puppy's parents, where possible, look for a pedigree, and read as much as you can about the breed of your choice. Go to the public library for reference sources on dogs, buy one of the many good books available, and go to dog shows and talk to the experts.

Most of these forty-five breeds are from the existing dog Groups as established by the American Kennel Club. AKC-registrable breeds fall into one of the following Groups: *Sporting Dogs, Hounds, Working Dogs, Terriers, Toys, Nonsporting Dogs, Herding Dogs*, plus the *Miscellaneous Class.* The breeds I recommend include dogs of every conceivable size, shape, temperament, and tendency. It should be clear by now that every household has different tastes, desires, and needs. You are certain to find at least one or two breeds that match up with your requirements. All the breeds portrayed here have in common a fondness for children. Beyond that they are as different as night and day. Read all the information you can about the breed you are most interested in, and pay close attention to descriptions of the dog's personality.

A brief word about the cost of a dog. Prices change quickly given frequent changes in the cost of living and other economic factors. Any price mentioned here may well change by the time you read this book. I do try to give you some indication of the cost of each breed. I use the categories of Moderate for dogs under $300, Expensive for dogs between $300 and $500, and Very expensive for dogs over $500. Please bear in mind that these prices will only be relevant for a short time. By the time you read this the prices will certainly have risen.

If the breed you are most interested in does not appear on these pages, that does not necessarily mean you should forget it. There are many reasonable breeders of those breeds not mentioned that produce lovable, adaptive dogs that maintain their original characteristics. Many breeds are not mentioned simply because of the limitation of space. But the sad truth is that many dogs of several breeds have been radically changed by poor breeding practices and/or mass breeding. There are no absolutes, however. One of the best Golden Retrievers I ever met many years ago was purchased from a pet shop. There are no rules to this game. You are at the mercy of pure luck although a diligent research effort can help to make a difference. To quote the grave marker of James Thurber's Airedale, Muggs, "Caveat Canem."

SPORTING DOGS

German Shorthaired Pointer

GERMAN SHORTHAIRED POINTER

Origin: The history of hunting dogs goes back long before written records were kept. In nineteenth-century Germany, hunters and breeders wanted to combine the separate abilities of the different hunting breeds—pointing, trailing, retrieving on land and water, keen scenting, hardy endurance—into one beautifully formed dog. After years of work and generations of breeding they produced the German Shorthaired Pointer. This breed is popular among nonhunters as well because German Shorthairs are particularly intelligent, loyal, and loving.

Height at shoulder: Males: 23 to 25 inches; females: 21 to 23 inches

Weight: Males: 35 to 70 pounds; females: 45 to 60 pounds

Grooming: There is some shedding but the coat is very short. A brushing now and then is good for the coat.

Cost: Moderate

Capabilities: German Shorthairs make wonderful watchdogs because they will bark at any strange sound. The German Shorthair is too gentle by nature for guard work. (A good guard dog must attack if needed.)

Training tip: Start early. As loving and loyal as this breed is, remember that this is a hunting dog. German Shorthairs need a very firm, strong, consistent hand from a very early age. They can be very strong-willed and stubborn without it.

Housebreaking: A breed so used to the outdoor life is more difficult to housebreak. Begin early, be firm, stick to a very rigid schedule, and don't be surprised over the years when mistakes happen. Get right back to the strict schedule and firm attitude.

Aesthetic quality: Brown and white athlete

Personality: Older children can appreciate the German Shorthair's friendship and faithfulness. Older children can also go on the long, long daily walks and runs necessary to keep this breed in even temper and good physical shape. Younger children would be overwhelmed. German Shorthairs need a lot of companionship. They hate to be left alone. Without enough exercise and company they can become destructive, chewing everything in reach and barking and howling till relief comes. City living is usually too confining for such an active hunting breed. Even with outdoor exercise the German Shorthair remains very active indoors. Many teenagers feel exactly the same way and enjoy playing chase and race with this handsome canine.

GOLDEN RETRIEVER

Origin: Goldens were bred like other retrievers in the nineteenth century by introducing various other breeds into their line. But the Golden was bred by Lord Tweedmouth's gamekeepers on his Scottish estate called Guisachan. A male yellow retriever named Nous was mated to a Tweed water spaniel named Belle in 1867 or 1868. From that romantic setting comes our present-day Golden Retriever.

Height at shoulder: Males: 23 to 24 inches; females: $21\frac{1}{2}$ to $22\frac{1}{2}$ inches

Weight: Males: 65 to 75 pounds; females: 60 to 70 pounds

Grooming: This beautiful, slightly wavy fur does shed. Regular brushing will help.

Cost: Expensive

Capabilities: The Golden is so easygoing and gentle that guarding is simply not in its nature. On the other hand, a Golden can be a totally trustworthy companion for a child. They often serve as guide dogs for the blind.

Training tip: This breed is extremely responsive. Training seems very easy because they are so willing to please. But these are hunting dogs whose minds can wander. Give commands and praise in a calm voice and be sure each command is obeyed properly.

Housebreaking: Retrievers are comparatively easy to housebreak.

Aesthetic quality: Honey-colored, graceful dogs with lovable faces

Personality: Goldens love everyone and understand everything. They are intelligent, dignified, considerate, and perfect for young children, toddlers, babies, or, of course, older children. That is not to say they are boring. If the child wants to play ball or run or just be silly, the Golden can do that too. Goldens can adjust to

Golden Retriever

almost any lifestyle in the city or the country, but they deserve to get some daily exercise and a swim now and then.

LABRADOR RETRIEVER

Origin: Like several other retrievers, the Labrador comes from Newfoundland. A real mystery is how Labrador Retrievers originally came to Newfoundland. They must have arrived by ship, since there were apparently no native dogs on the American continent. But such records were never kept. In the mid–nineteenth century, the earl of Malmesbury and the duke of Buceleuch each sponsored the breeding of pure Labradors in England. If not for the English, we would not have these magnificent dogs. They all but disappeared from Newfoundland when a dog tax was imposed in the late nineteenth century.

Height at shoulder: Males: $22\frac{1}{2}$ to $24\frac{1}{2}$ inches; females: $21\frac{1}{2}$ to $23\frac{1}{2}$ inches

Weight: Males: 60 to 75 pounds; females: 55 to 70 pounds

Grooming: This shiny, short, close-lying, black or yellow coat sheds a little but not excessively. Brushing is helpful. Retrievers love water, so baths can be fun.

Cost: Moderate

Labrador Retriever

Capabilities: Labradors are amazingly versatile dogs. Of course, they hunt and retrieve but they also make good guard dogs and watchdogs while remaining gentle and trustworthy with children. Many Labs have been trained as guide dogs for the blind.

Training tip: Training such an intelligent animal is easy, providing the trainer stays in charge. The Labrador's intelligence can make him mischievous if he is not controlled. Demand a lot from a breed with so much potential, and begin early. Give them generous praise.

Housebreaking: Begin early and stick to the schedule. Some Labradors make a mistake now and then and some don't.

Aesthetic quality: Staunch, powerful dignity

Personality: Labs are as intelligent, devoted, reliable, and even tempered as a dog can be. They are active indoors and need to run outdoors and yet they can adjust well to city life. They are large, assertive dogs that relate very well to toddlers and young children as well as to older children. They love to retrieve balls and sticks and are expert swimmers. After all, they worked for fishermen in their Newfoundland days.

ENGLISH SETTER

Origin: Bird dogs have been very important to the English hunter throughout their history. Four hundred years ago, the English Setter was bred from various spaniels, including the Spanish Pointer. In addition to its superb skill in the field, the English Setter has an extraordinary beauty. Though it is seen in solid colors or a solid color and white, it is most recognizable in its "belton" coat (white with flecks or freckles of the darker color).

Height at shoulder: Males: 25 inches; females: 24 inches

Weight: Males: 60 to 70 pounds; females: 50 to 60 pounds

Grooming: The English Setter's flat, straight coat needs expert trimming now and then. Frequent brushing keeps the coat in good condition. There is some shedding.

Cost: Moderate

English Setter

Capabilities: The English Setter's greatest trait is patience. They have an easygoing laid-back quality not suited to guard work, though they can sometimes function as watchdogs.

Training tip: In training, the English Setter's patience can become stubborn resistance. Try coaxing, insistence, and ecstatic praise. Never get tough with an English Setter. It doesn't work. Begin early and always be firm and consistent.

Housebreaking: Setters are not easy to housebreak. Begin early, stick closely to the schedule, and always praise the successes. Admonish the failures but don't use punishment. Begin immediately with housebreaking and skip paper-training. The transition from paper-training to housebreaking would only serve to confuse the dog.

Aesthetic quality: Magnificent form and grace on point or in motion; color, pattern, and texture are glorious

Personality: Affectionate, loving, gentle English Setters are quiet and relaxed inside, but require long, vigorous runs outside every day. They also require undying love and devotion from every member of the family. They can be remarkably patient with toddlers and young children or they can give big kids a run for their money. Adjustment to apartment life is quite good.

GORDON SETTER

Origin: In the late eighteenth century, the duke of Gordon gave his name to an already existing black and mahogany setter. The duke developed the breed to locate birds in the field at his castle in Scotland. In the middle of the nineteenth century, the Gordon Setter and its expertise were brought to America.

Gordon Setter

Height at shoulder: Males: 24 to 27 inches; females: 23 to 26 inches

Weight: Males: 55 to 80 pounds; females: 45 to 70 pounds

Grooming: The Gordon Setter's flat, slightly wavy coat sometimes needs expert trimming. There is some shedding. Regular brushing helps.

Cost: Moderate

Capabilities: Unlike the other setters, Gordons can be trained to guard. They have a more protective nature than the English or the Irish Setter, but they retain the setter's love of children.

Training tip: Begin early and be very firm. The Gordon is stubborn. Habits once established are difficult to break.

Housebreaking: Try not to paper-train Gordons. The transition to housebreaking is confusing for them. They have the typical setter difficulty with housebreaking. Stick to rigid schedules and begin early.

Aesthetic quality: Strength and great dignity in a black and tan coat

Personality: Gordons are hunting dogs and usually do best in the country. With long outdoor runs, they can settle down when they come inside. Like the other setters, the Gordon likes a lot of attention from its family and in return takes excellent care of all the children from infancy to adulthood.

IRISH SETTER

Origin: This easily recognized Irishman was created at the beginning of the eighteenth century in Ireland. It was red and white then, and still is in Ireland. It is bred strictly for that solid mahogany-red color in America only.

Height at shoulder: Males: 27 inches; females: 25 inches

Irish Setter

Weight: Males: 70 pounds; females: 60 pounds

Grooming: The flat, straight setter coat needs expert trimming now and then. There is some shedding. Regular brushing keeps the dog in good condition.

Cost: Expensive

Capabilities: In addition to their hunting talents, Irish Setters are good entertainers. They are very playful and like to clown around. Guard work is out of the question, but some Irish Setters are good watchdogs.

Training tip: Begin early and be very firm. The Irish Setter shows that typical setter stubbornness.

Housebreaking: The Irish Setter, like his fellow setters, requires a strict housebreaking schedule. Begin with housebreaking as early as possible. Skip paper-training: it causes confusion. Be firm, consistent, and diligent.

Aesthetic quality: Shining, breathtaking, chestnut red coat

Personality: Without training, the Irish Setter can be much too playful for very young children. They are big dogs who like to romp and play with big kids. This is not a sedate dog. Irish Setters love and need miles of outdoor exercise every day. Once inside after exercise they remain very active for the rest of the day. A country setting is best for them.

Brittany Spaniel

BRITTANY SPANIEL

Origin: The "French" spaniel is véry popular at field trials. Brittanys resemble setters as much as spaniels, but the Brittany's tail is always short, like those of its fellow spaniels. Unlike other spaniels, though, the Brittany is often born with a short tail. Brittanys were used to hunt woodcock in western France long before records were kept.

Height at shoulder: Males and females: 17½ to 20½ inches

Weight: Males and females: 30 to 40 pounds

Grooming: These spaniels shed a little. They need regular brushing and an occasional trim.

Cost: Moderate

Capabilities: These hunters are warm, friendly companion dogs that can serve as watchdogs because they will bark at outside sounds and intruders. Although more assertive than the other spaniels, they are not suitable for guard work.

Training tip: Brittanys respond to obedience training a little more readily than some of the other hunting breeds, but they still need an early beginning, a firm hand, a consistent routine, and a strong-willed trainer.

Housebreaking: Housebreaking goes pretty well considering this is a hunting dog, but begin early and be consistent.

Aesthetic quality: Tall, orange or brown and white spaniel

Personality: If given enough outdoor exercise, Brittanys do well in the city. They love children and play well with them. But since they are large dogs and quite active even inside, they would probably overwhelm most toddlers. All Brittanys are affectionate, gentle, and outgoing. Occasionally, a Brittany will become attached to one person in a family. Have everyone get involved with the dog's daily routine to avoid singular attachments.

Clumber Spaniel

CLUMBER SPANIEL

Origin: The dukes of Newcastle lived in Clumber Park, Nottingham. As far back as the nineteenth century, they bred an uncharacteristic spaniel from various dogs imported from France. Clumber Spaniels are shaped like spaniel cousins of the Basset Hound and have an excellent nose for finding game. Clumbers made their appearance in America in 1883.

Height at shoulder: Males and females: 16 to 19 inches

Weight: Males: 55 to 65 pounds; females: 35 to 50 pounds

Grooming: These spaniels shed a little. They need regular brushing and an occasional trim.

Cost: Expensive

Capabilities: They're good hunters, but don't look for a guard dog or a watchdog here.

Training tip: Clumbers give leisurely responses. Just begin early, be patient and consistent, and don't give up.

Housebreaking: This chore goes pretty well. Stick to the schedule.

Aesthetic quality: Heavyset, cartoonlike face

Personality: Clumbers never seem to be in much of a hurry. Outdoor exercise is important, but they would just as soon wait till tomorrow. Small apartments are fine despite the dogs' size since they have such sedate temperaments. A Clumber is affectionate and gentle and a tower of patience with toddlers and small children. He can become attached to one person, so encourage everyone in the family to relate to him every day. His style of play is very subtle. Clumbers need to be coaxed.

COCKER SPANIEL

Origin: The always popular and easily recognizable Cocker (often called the American Cocker) is one of the smaller breeds of the ancient spaniels. The Cocker Spaniel takes its name from the woodcock, which it can find, flush, and retrieve so well. The breed was introduced in America in the 1880s. By the middle of the twentieth century, the Cocker Spaniel had become one of the most popular and prolific breeds in the country. After suffering some breeding problems as a result of indiscriminate mass production, the Cocker Spaniel is now regaining its deserved position as an ideal American dog.

Height at shoulder: Males: 14½ to 15½ inches; females: 13½ to 14½ inches

Weight: Males: 25 to 28 pounds; females: 23 to 26 pounds

Grooming: Cocker Spaniels shed. They need regular brushing and trimming by an expert.

Cost: Moderate

Cocker Spaniel

Capabilities: Cockers are not meant to be guard dogs, but they can make good watchdogs.

Training tip: These are bright, responsive animals. Because they are essentially hunting dogs, it is a good idea to begin training them early. Resist their irresistible expressions and demand obedience to all your commands. Cockers respond very poorly to physical abuse. Always avoid hitting, but especially with a Cocker.

Housebreaking: A good reason for sticking to obedience training is because it helps with housebreaking. Hunting breeds, and the Cocker is a hunting breed, have lived outdoors in kennels for so many generations that controlling bodily functions when indoors can be difficult. Begin housebreaking early and stick to a schedule. Praise success. Admonish failure but without physical abuse, including rolled-up newspapers.

Aesthetic quality: Sweet, small dog with big, hanging ears and big, gentle eyes

Personality: A well-bred Cocker can live happily in a city apartment. Given a fair amount of outdoor exercise, it will remain even tempered and moderately active indoors. Cockers are gentle, cheerful, and easy to get along with. They are wonderful companions for children of all ages. Just be sure to get a well-bred puppy. A large family would do well with a Cocker because the dog can give personal attention, love, and play to each member.

English Cocker Spaniel

ENGLISH COCKER SPANIEL

Origin: The English Cocker is slightly larger than the American Cocker and is closely related to the English Springer Spaniel. The English began to breed spaniels separately by size in the late nineteenth century, but they all retain that splendid, engaging spaniel personality.

Height at shoulder: Males: 16 to 17 inches; females: 15 to 16 inches

Weight: Males: 28 to 34 pounds; females: 26 to 32 pounds

Grooming: English Cockers shed. They need regular brushing and expert trimming.

Cost: Moderate

Capabilities: Anyone should be able to get along with an English Cocker, including an intruder. However, Cockers will bark at strange noises or when someone comes to the door, making them effective watchdogs.

Training tip: This breed trains rather easily, especially for a hunting breed. They are responsive and willing to please if the trainer is consistent and firm.

Housebreaking: Patience may be required. Stick to rigid schedules, begin early, praise successes. Scold them, but never hit them for failures.

Aesthetic quality: Long, hanging ears and graceful sporting lines

Personality: Marvelous, adaptive English Cockers can do well in either the country or the city as long as they get some outdoor exercise. They are moderately active indoors, certainly active enough to show a houseful of children a good time. English Cockers are well suited to children of all ages. They are so adaptive and loving that any child flourishes in their presence.

ENGLISH SPRINGER SPANIEL

Origin: These spaniels are named for their ability to "spring" a bird from cover, forcing it to fly up. The smaller Cockers flush the woodcock, a low-flying bird. Springers and Cockers are considered land spaniels, though both can retrieve from water if needed.

Height at shoulder: Males: 20 inches; females: 19 inches

English Springer Spaniel

Weight: Males: 49 to 55 pounds; females: 46 to 50 pounds

Grooming: English Springers shed. They need regular brushing and expert trimming.

Cost: Moderate

Capabilities: Springers can serve as watchdogs but not guard dogs. They are expert hunters and companions.

Training tip: English Springers respond well for a hunting breed. They are eager to please and are responsive. Take advantage of their responsiveness and give them a good, consistent, early obedience course.

Housebreaking: Typical hunting dog difficulties with housebreaking occur in this breed, too. A conscientious obedience course can help. Begin housebreaking early and stick to a schedule.

Aesthetic quality: Long, hanging ears and graceful sporting lines

Personality: These are good city or country dogs. They are active and need exercise, the kind a group of children can give them. Though they are larger than other spaniels, easygoing Springers are usually gentle with toddlers and playful with older children. Like all spaniels, they love retrieving balls and sticks.

Weimaraner

WEIMARANER

Origin: Another magnificent German hunting dog created by dedicated breeders in the nineteenth century, the Weimaraner, named for the court at Weimar, was bred to hunt large game such as wolf, bear, deer, and wildcat. There is no large game to hunt in Germany now, and little elsewhere for that matter, so the Weimaraner has been adapted to bird hunting, which suits the breed equally well.

Height at shoulder: Males: 25 to 27 inches; females: 23 to 25 inches

Weight: Males: 70 to 85 pounds; females: 55 to 70 pounds

Grooming: There is some shedding but the coat is short. Periodic brushing is good for the dog's coat.

Cost: Moderate

Capabilities: Weimaraners make wonderful watchdogs. They will sound the alarm at any unfamiliar noise. Many of them can be trained to guard and attack, but such training requires an expert. These dogs do not guard naturally, and, if trained to do so, need constant supervision.

Training tip: Begin early, very early; be firm; be consistent; never waver. These are hunting dogs who have been bred to follow their own instincts, not those of their owners. Unless the owner wants the dog to track a mountain lion or bring a wild pheasant home for dinner, there may be a conflict of interests. Teach this breed from the beginning that the owner makes all the decisions and must be obeyed every time.

Housebreaking: Hunting breeds accustomed to outdoor living are difficult to housebreak. Weimaraners must begin early, be given rigid schedules, and be firmly corrected.

Aesthetic quality: Sleek, iridescent gray hunter

Personality: These dogs are bright and develop very personal relationships with each member of the family. They are wonderful for older children who have the time and energy to give them long, daily runs and lots of active personal attention. Weimaraners are very active indoors, as well, so they are not well suited to a sedentary household or to city living. Small children usually find the Weimaraner too large and too active to play with comfortably.

HOUNDS

BASSET HOUND

Origin: *Bas* in French means a "low thing" or "dwarf." A dog referred to as a Basset was mentioned in a 1585 French treatise on badger hunting. But the Basset Hound appears to have been used most often for hunting rabbits, hares, and deer in France and Belgium. The Basset Hound looks like a Bloodhound on short legs and shares that dog's ability to follow a scent.

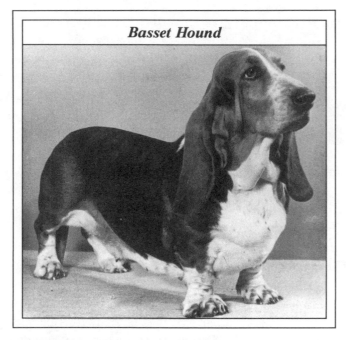

Basset Hound

Height at shoulder: Males and females: 14 inches
Weight: Males and females: 45 pounds
Grooming: This breed sheds, but at least the coat is short.
   Otherwise, they just need an occasional brushing.
Cost: Moderate

Capabilities: Creating a quiet, relaxed atmosphere is one of the Basset's most noticeable qualities, but it will act as watchdog if no one else will do it. Guarding is out. They are much too easygoing for guard work.

Training tip: Bassets are very responsive. Just don't expect quick responses. Give them more praise than correction. Flattery will get you everywhere.

Housebreaking: Early obedience training along with early housebreaking are the best insurance. Some Basset Hounds do have trouble with this chore.

Aesthetic quality: Long, low, heavy, and calm, with a deadpan expression

Personality: Cooperative, gentle, cheerful Bassets need their family's attention and love. They are not very active indoors but deserve a good walk outdoors, which makes them ideal for the city. Toddlers are handled with the patience of Job and quiet older children will value the loyalty and friendship offered by a Basset. Only a very active teenager might be disappointed when the dog prefers a game of Scrabble to a game of catch.

BEAGLE

Origin: The Romans found Beagle packs in England when they arrived. The English used Beagles for hunting rabbits. Beagle means *small*, for they are the smallest of the hounds. Although they have been bred for centuries in packs, they adapt well to living individually with families. The Beagle that we see today in America was developed in the 1880s. They are bred in two varieties, different only in size. The 13-inch variety and the 15-inch variety both resemble the English Foxhound in miniature and both participate in AKC Beagle field trials.

Beagle

Variety 1

Height at shoulder: Males and females: not to exceed 13
   inches
Weight: Males and females: 15 to 20 pounds

Variety 2

Height at shoulder: Males and females: 13 to 15 inches
Weight: Males and females: 18 to 23 pounds

Grooming: Beagles shed a bit, but the coat is short. Occasional brushing is recommended.
Cost: Moderate
Capabilities: Announcing the approach of strangers is
   well within the Beagle's talents, though protection is
   not.
Training tip: Circumvent an inborn stubbornness by be-

ginning training early. Give a lot of praise and demand a lot. Be firm but never punish. Beagles respond very poorly to punishment.

Housebreaking: Housebreaking is difficult if begun late. Get an early start and there will be no problem. Rigid schedules always help.

Aesthetic quality: The "Snoopy" look

Personality: There is a reason why Beagles are so popular. They are sweet-natured dogs that seem to be genuinely happy. However, the Beagle's popularity has led to indiscriminate breeding, so be sure to get a well-bred puppy. Beagles hate to be left alone. They need a lot of outdoor exercise and are fairly active indoors, but many have made a smooth adjustment to apartment living. They are gentle enough for toddlers and playful enough for older children.

BLACK AND TAN COONHOUND

Origin: Black and Tans are scent hounds; they live by their noses. They have been bred from English Talbot Hounds, Bloodhounds, and Foxhounds to create a dog that is capable of hunting by scent and that possesses a beautiful black and tan coat. Obviously, these hounds specialize in hunting raccoons, but they also excel in trailing deer, mountain lions, and bears.

Height at shoulder: Males: 25 to 27 inches; females: 23 to 25 inches

Weight: Males: 65 to 85 pounds; females: 60 to 80 pounds

Grooming: There is some shedding of the short coat. The dog needs a brushing now and then.

Cost: Moderate

Capabilities: Black and Tans can function as watchdogs and occasionally as guard dogs, although it is not their primary talent. They are primarily scenting hounds.

Training tip: These are responsive dogs. Do not be too exuberant when praising them. They need to concentrate.

Housebreaking: They have surprisingly few problems in this area, but don't take a hound for granted.

Aesthetic quality: Sleek, athletic hunting dog

Black and Tan Coonhound

Personality: This is a large, energetic animal that needs extensive, daily outdoor exercise, which usually means a country setting is best. However, he is calm indoors. Such a large, active dog would seem to be too much for a toddler, but if the child doesn't mind, the Black and Tan doesn't. They are very patient, easygoing members of the family. What they don't like is being left alone.

Irish Wolfhound

IRISH WOLFHOUND

Origin: This medieval giant of Ireland hunted the elk (six feet at the shoulder) and the wolf for kings. There is even mention of this enormous dog in Roman history. But by the nineteenth century the Irish Wolfhound was almost extinct. The breed was saved by a Scottish officer in the British army, Captain George A. Graham.

Height at shoulder: Males: 32 to 34 inches; females: 30 to 32 inches

Weight: Males: at least 120 pounds; females: at least 105 pounds

Grooming: This wiry, rough coat needs regular brushing, trimming, and stripping (plucking out loose fur with one's fingers). There is also some shedding.

Cost: Very expensive

Capabilities: They are beautiful to look at and easy to live with. They are not suitable as watchdogs or guard dogs.

Training tip: Be firm. These dogs must be controlled because of their size. A consistent, early beginning represents the best approach. Irish Wolfhounds will respond quite well when they know you mean it.

Housebreaking: Irish Wolfhounds have no problem with housebreaking, but begin early.

Aesthetic quality: Lovable, smiling giant

Personality: They do not like to rush. Wolfhounds are easygoing, cooperative dogs who must be pushed to take their long daily gallops. Being inactive indoors, they adapt well to city life. Older children are better suited to the Irish Wolfhound. Small children might be overcome by the dog's size. They are especially good at rough play with big kids. These very large dogs have shorter life spans than smaller breeds.

Otter Hound

OTTER HOUND

Origin: From the early thirteenth century on, there was a need in England to hunt otter. People and otter were in competition for fish. In the nineteenth century otter hunting became a sport, and Otter Hounds were kept in packs. But most of the otters in England are gone now, as are most of the Otter Hounds. The dog's happy-go-lucky quality is beginning to appeal to Americans.

Height at shoulder: Males: 24 to 27 inches; females: 22 to 26 inches

Weight: Males: 75 to 115 pounds; females: 65 to 100 pounds

Grooming: The rough, shaggy coat needs some care and brushing to keep that tousled look. There is shedding.

Cost: Moderate

Capabilities: These are happy, friendly dogs who do a little watching but no guarding.

Training tip: Otter Hounds are difficult to train. Be firm and consistent. Begin early and stay with it. Training is important for such a large dog.

Housebreaking: Keep rigid schedules and be very firm. Housebreaking an Otter Hound is difficult. Begin early.

Aesthetic quality: Playful, shaggy giant

Personality: The ancient but rare Otter Hound is best suited to country living. They are happy, easygoing dogs who love everyone, but they should never be off leash or out of the owner's control. They will take off after a wild animal and wonder where they are miles later. Big children have a great time with these big dogs, but small children need a different breed.

WORKING DOGS

BERNESE MOUNTAIN DOG

Origin: Named for the canton of Bern in Switzerland, this canine serves the Swiss farmer by herding, pulling loads, and guarding the farmhouse and stock. The Bernese has been closely identified with the basket weavers of the canton of Bern for centuries, helping transport their shipments to market. Progenitors of the breed were brought to Switzerland by the Romans. Selective breeding was not begun until the end of the eighteenth century. These large, stately animals sport heavy, medium-length fur. They can be comfortable outdoors through an entire winter but they need the closeness of their families.

Height at shoulder: Males: 23 to 27½ inches; females: 21 to 26 inches

Weight: Males: 80 to 105 pounds; females: 75 to 90 pounds

Grooming: The Bernese does shed, though not excessively. A good brushing once or twice a week will keep its coat in good shape.

Cost: Expensive

Capabilities: An owner can ask a Bernese to guard the house and children, to warn of approaching strangers, to haul loads on a cart, or to sit back and play with the kids and have a good time.

Training tip: These dogs are very intelligent and sensitive. They do not need harsh or loud corrections. A gentle voice and a patient manner will work wonders. Praise them as soon as they have obeyed a command and be generous with the praise. Training need not begin at a terribly early age, but socializing should. The puppies are adorable and should get a lot of human companionship as early as possible.

Bernese Mountain Dog

Housebreaking: No problem

Aesthetic quality: Big, sturdy, black dog with a white face and chest

Personality: Children of any age will be ecstatically happy with a Bernese Mountain Dog. These dogs tend to lean on someone they love. If that someone is a small child, some supervision might be necessary. The Bernese is gentle, even tempered, and patient. People outside the dog's immediate family are usually ignored. This breed deserves a decent amount of outdoor exercise but remains reasonably relaxed and quiet indoors, so it does well in the city.

BOXER

Origin: Boxers get their name from the fact that they tend to begin a fight by swinging their front paws. They were bred to fight hundreds of years ago. The breed as we now know it was developed long ago in Germany

Boxer

through crossing Bulldogs, terriers, probably Great Danes, and Mastiffs. After bullbaiting and dog fights were outlawed in the middle of the nineteenth century, the Boxer was used in police and guard work. It still makes a fine guard dog, but its viciousness has been bred out in the twentieth century. Thus, the Boxer makes an excellent, affectionate pet.

Height at shoulder: Males: $22\frac{1}{2}$ to 25 inches; females: 21 to $23\frac{1}{2}$ inches

Weight: Males: 60 to 70 pounds; females: 50 to 60 pounds

Grooming: Care of the Boxer is easy. There is some shedding, but the coat is short. An occasional brushing helps.

Cost: Moderate

Capabilities: Clearly, the Boxer is an excellent guard dog and companion. He is also a good watchdog.

Training tip: Boxers can be stubborn if training begins too late. Begin early, at about three months old.

Housebreaking: These dogs are easily housebroken when taught early in life.

Aesthetic quality: Majestic stance and wise expression

Personality: Boxers have intelligent, dominant personalities but surprisingly enough get along well with children. They love to play and romp with older kids. Most little children would have a hard time holding their own. Both the city and the country suit this breed. They are moderately active indoors and out. Boxers are very popular, so look for a well-bred puppy.

Great Dane

GREAT DANE

Origin: This giant breed was mentioned in eighteenth-century European animal studies and most likely existed before that. It was used to hunt the ferocious wild boar. The French called it the Great Dane (grand Danois), although the dog does not have any connection with Denmark. Concentrated breed development of the Great Dane took place in Germany in the nineteenth century where it is called *Deutsche dogge* (German Mastiff).

Height at shoulder: Males: no less than 30 inches; females: no less than 28 inches

Weight: Males: 135 to 150 pounds; females: 120 to 135 pounds

Grooming: Occasional brushing is all a Dane needs. There is some shedding but the coat is short.

Cost: Expensive

Capabilities: Danes make good watchdogs but not guard dogs.

Training tip: Sometimes sensitive, sometimes stubborn, these dogs need a lot of praise. Be gentle and coaxing, not harsh.

Housebreaking: They housebreak well if taught early.

Aesthetic quality: Majestic, graceful, and dignified

Personality: Danes must be exercised outdoors every day whether they feel like it or not. Most living situations will do because Danes are so easy and agreeable. They do well in the city and can even adapt to small apartments, but more space is desirable. Children could have trouble with the dog's desire to lean on those he likes: a child cannot support a 150-pound dog. But if the dog is taught not to lean from the very beginning, the problem can be avoided. These are not very active dogs, so they are good with small children. Very large dogs such as Great Danes have shorter life spans than smaller dogs.

Newfoundland

NEWFOUNDLAND

Origin: This breed was developed on the northeastern Canadian island of Newfoundland to help the fishermen with their nets, save victims of shipwrecks, haul heavy loads, and protect children. The "Neuf" performs all of these tasks to perfection. There is no record of what dogs went into the breeding of the Newfoundland several hundred years ago, but they must have been imported because there were no dogs native to the American continent at that time.

Height at shoulder: Males: 28 inches; females: 26 inches

Weight: Males: 150 pounds; females: 120 pounds

Grooming: This breed has a medium-long outercoat and a heavy undercoat, both of which shed year-round. In the late spring and early fall they shed heavily to prepare for the new season. A lot of brushing is necessary.

Cost: Expensive

Capabilities: Technically, Newfoundlands are not guard
dogs because they won't naturally protect buildings or
boundaries, but they will usually come to the protection
of children. Neufs are truly canine nannies. They can
also function as watchdogs.

Training tip: The Newfoundland is very responsive and
willing to please, so training should not be difficult. Be
gentle and patient. This breed is very sensitive to harsh
treatment; it makes them shy. They respond best to
generous praise.

Housebreaking: No problem

Aesthetic quality: A massive, black bear

Personality: Although they are quite large, Newfoundlands are splendid with toddlers as well as older kids.
Neufs are always affectionate. They love water almost as
much as they love their families. If possible, swimming
is the best exercise for these big, happy, reliable dogs.
Such a large animal needs a large home, but it can be in
the city or the country. Like most large breeds, they are
inactive indoors and have a reduced life expectancy.

SAMOYED

Origin: The Samoyed people live near Finland in north-
west Russia with their happy, laughing, white dogs. The
people and the dogs have lived in the same place for
longer than recorded history. Over the years, these dogs
have cheerfully performed such duties as herding reindeer, pulling heavy loads on sleds, and protecting their
families. This robust dog is much admired for its sump-
tuous white fur.

Height at shoulder: Males: 21 to 23½ inches; females: 19
to 21 inches

Weight: Males: 50 to 75 pounds; females: 40 to 55 pounds

Grooming: The medium-length outercoat and the heavy undercoat shed all year-round. In late spring and early fall they shed heavily to prepare for the change of season. This heavy shedding is a form of natural dry cleaning for these white dogs. Northern dogs have strong, rather resistant coats that tend to stay cleaner than the coats of other breeds. If they have romped through mud,

Samoyed

just clean the dirty area and keep the regular baths to a minimum. Regular brushing to remove loose fur is the most important grooming task.

Cost: Moderate

Capabilities: The Samoyed is a good watchdog but not a protection dog. They do like to pull sleds.

Training tip: They like to pull people, too. Training must begin early. These are strong, stubborn dogs that need convincing. They ignore punishment, so firm, consistent obedience training is very important.

Housebreaking: Begin early and stick to the schedule rigidly. Be patient. Reward success every time; admonish failures, but don't bother punishing. Although Samoyeds have trouble with housebreaking, they eventually succeed.

Aesthetic quality: Luxurious, thick white fur coat

Personality: The Samoyed is a very happy, playful, active animal. He is slightly calmer than the Siberian Husky, so he is better for younger children as long as there is supervision. Samoyeds are happiest in large apartments or houses. This dog needs a lot of exercise both inside and out, but he does seem to do well in the city.

Siberian Husky

SIBERIAN HUSKY

Origin: The Chukchi natives bred the Siberian Husky to pull sleds over the long expanses of snow and ice in northeast Russia. These dogs work in teams to pull light loads over incredible distances. They are very popular at sled dog races in the United States and Canada.

Height at shoulder: Males: 21 to 23½ inches; females: 20 to 22 inches

Weight: Males: 45 to 60 pounds; females: 35 to 50 pounds

Grooming: The harsh outercoat and the heavy undercoat shed throughout the year. In the late spring and early fall they shed heavily to prepare for the new season. The heavy shedding and the dog's natural habit of cleaning himself somewhat like a cat make frequent baths unnecessary.

Cost: Moderate

Capabilities: Pulling sleds and playing are the Siberian's talents. Protection work is out of the question. They don't even bark; they howl.

Training tip: Siberians are very stubborn and playful. Be firm, authoritative, and consistent. Begin training early and give firm corrections. This is a very strong breed.

Housebreaking: This chore is sometimes difficult. Siberians need frequent walks, strict schedules, and an early beginning. They are impervious to punishment, but strict adherence to an obedience course will create the self-discipline necessary for successful housebreaking.

Aesthetic quality: Mischievous wolf

Personality: These happy, happy dogs need to run, play, and see people and lots of children. They are energetic, medium-sized dogs that seldom calm down. Small children would be overwhelmed. Huskies hate to be left alone. Huskies do best in large apartments or houses where there is room for all that energy. Still, many huskies have adjusted to city life.

TERRIERS

Airedale

AIREDALE

Origin: The old English Terriers were bred to hunt fox, rats, weasels, and other nuisance rodents in the English countryside. In the early nineteenth century, these terriers were bred with the popular Otter Hound to combine the superior eyesight and hearing of the terrier and the superior scenting ability of the Otter Hound all in one hardy, courageous dog. The cross was so successful that the resulting Airedale (named for the Aire Valley) was shown in its own competition in 1879 at the Airedale Agricultural Society Show. The breed has flourished ever since because Airedales can adjust to so many different lifestyles. They are the largest of the terriers and perhaps more restrained than some of their cousins.

Height at shoulder: Males: 23 inches; females: 22 inches

Weight: Males: 50 to 60 pounds; females: 45 to 55 pounds

Grooming: The rough, wiry quality of the terrier coat needs very little care. The softer undercoat will periodically loosen to make way for new growth. Those with the time and patience should hand pluck out the loose, dead undercoat by pulling the tufts between the thumb and forefinger. However, those with a busier schedule can take the dog to a professional groomer to be trimmed and clipped. Except for the loosened undercoat, which stays on the body till plucked, there is very little shedding. Regular brushing is a good idea.

Cost: Moderate

Capabilities: The tenacious quality needed to hunt rats and the loyal hound spirit have made the Airedale an excellent guard dog. These dogs have been used by the military and the police because they will execute their commands even when wounded. Airedales are courageous, indefatigable hunters and trusted companions.

Training tip: When Airedales are trained as young puppies they learn quickly, easily, and willingly. They accept human dominance at this early age, which is important. If allowed to go untrained, an Airedale can become stubborn and difficult to control. This strong, independent spirit always needs a firm, decisive trainer.

Housebreaking: Well-taught puppies become well-housebroken dogs.

Aesthetic quality: Dominant, alert dignity

Personality: Older children have a great time with Airedales. These dogs can run and jump and wrestle endlessly. But fifty pounds of boundless joy is too much for younger children. Airedales like to run and play a lot inside and outside until a stranger comes along; then the dogs become aloof and distant. Airedales are territorial and may fight with strange dogs. Therefore they require early obedience training. They are usually polite to outsiders, both people and dogs, unless attacked. If they or their families are attacked, they are fearless. Despite the high energy level, this breed adapts well to a city lifestyle.

BORDER TERRIER

Origin: Farmers along the border of Scotland and northern England have been plagued by hill foxes for hundreds of years. The farmers' defense is the Border Terrier. They

Border Terrier

are tough little dogs who can hunt and kill a fox—no
small feat. This breed may be difficult but not impossible to obtain. The American Kennel Club can be of
help in locating a breeder. The dog is more commonly
found in England and Scotland.

Height at shoulder: Males: 13 to 14 inches; females: 11 to
12 inches

Weight: Males: 13 to 15½ pounds; females: 11½ to 14
pounds

Grooming: The wiry topcoat and soft undercoat shed a
little, but regular brushing is all that is needed.

Cost: Moderate

Capabilities: Borders make good little watchdogs. They
are too small for guarding but they make excellent
ratters.

Training tip: These are responsive dogs, especially for a
terrier. They do not respond well to harsh treatment: it
could make them timid. Give them praise and encouragement and be consistent.

Housebreaking: Like most terriers, this one should not
have housebreaking problems.

Aesthetic quality: Scrappy, scruffy little tough guy

Personality: Borders are the most calm of the terriers
while still maintaining the terrier personality, which
makes them ideal for children, young and old. Borders
do not like to sit around, though. They are very active
dogs indoors as well as out. City life is fine if they get
enough exercise and if they are introduced to the noise
and hubbub as puppies.

CAIRN TERRIER

Origin: The Cairn stems from the Isle of Skye and the
West Highlands of Scotland, as does the West Highland
White Terrier. A very specific description for the Cairn

Cairn Terrier

existed by the middle of the nineteenth century. These little terriers are all wonderful, feisty hunters of rodents and small game. Dorothy's Toto was a Cairn who was typically devoted to his mistress as they searched for the mythical land of Oz. Cairns are very partial to their own families and indifferent to "outsiders." The spirit of a two-and-a-half-year-old is retained for a lifetime in this breed. However, the Cairn may not want to share that particular spotlight with a two-and-a-half-year-old human. Older children can get along with a Cairn much better.

Height at shoulder: Males: 10 inches; females: 9½ inches

Weight: Males: 14 pounds; females: 13 pounds

Grooming: Caring for Cairns is easy. They have the rough outercoat and the soft undercoat of the terrier. Now and then that undercoat needs to be plucked (the loose hair pulled out with the thumb and forefinger). Regular brushing is recommended.

Cost: Moderate

Capabilities: Just as they would threaten rodents and foxes hiding in the rocks, they will warn of strangers at the door. They are small and thus unsuited to actual guard work, contrary to what they may think. A Cairn's self-image is quite sound.

Training tip: Cairns are terriers. They are stubborn and sometimes aggressive. So begin training early and be patient. Be firm and be consistent; don't let them get away without obeying every command just because they are adorable.

Housebreaking: Some little dogs are difficult to housebreak, but not this one. A Cairn is a neat, tidy little animal. Just show him what to do.

Aesthetic quality: Little tough guy

Personality: All Cairns love their families and are very devoted to the members of their own household. Some Cairns enjoy company, even a houseful of strangers, but some do not. They can live happily in a city apartment or they can run loose over a large estate. Adaptability is a trademark of this intelligent breed. Certainly, they are splendid with older children. With younger children, some Cairns are too feisty, too scrappy. Then again, some young children are too feisty for a little dog. As tough as the Cairn is, he is not a big-boned tower of patience. He can't take the indiscriminate pounding some very small children might mete out.

FOX TERRIER (SMOOTH AND WIRE)

Origin: Both varieties of Fox Terrier were bred from other terriers in nineteenth-century England. Fox Terriers were used with packs of Foxhounds. After the larger Foxhounds ran a fox to ground, the Fox Terrier would burrow into the tunnel for the kill. As foxhunting waned, the Fox Terrier became more popular in the showring and in high-fashion settings. Remember Asta in the *Thin Man* movies?

Height at shoulder: Males: not to exceed 15½ inches; females: proportionately shorter than males

Weight: Males: 17 to 19 pounds; females: 15 to 17 pounds

Grooming: There is little shedding. But the wirehaired variety needs regular brushing plus visits to the professional groomer for clipping. The smooth variety needs a brushing only now and then.

Fox Terrier (Wire)

Cost: Moderate

Capabilities: These are wonderful watchdogs. They will bark at any sound or unusual circumstance. But they are not guard dogs.

Training tip: Begin early. Be consistent and firm. This breed is bright and responsive if the training is very consistent. When a Fox Terrier is given his own way, his stubborn streak begins to show.

Housebreaking: Some Fox Terriers have more difficulty with housebreaking than others. Don't wait to find out. Begin training early and be firm.

Aesthetic quality: Alert, clever, and playful

Personality: They need busy, active, older children who want to play. A Fox Terrier's outdoor exercise does not have to consist of jogging, but he needs a lot of time to chase balls and to see what's going on. Such active dogs need a fair-sized home in the city or country. Be sure that the child and the dog understand that the child must be in charge at all times. Fox Terriers like to take over if given a chance. Small children are usually not dominant enough, fast enough, or alert enough to handle this breed. These dogs require a gentle but firm hand, plus one who can outwit them. They are very clever and quite stubborn. They can make you laugh at their tricks and frown at their scrappiness. They are wonderful for older kids and teenagers.

SOFT-COATED WHEATEN TERRIER

Origin: This terrier with the unusual fluffy fur comes from Ireland. From all accounts it was a dependable farm dog, protecting livestock and hunting small vermin for hundreds of years while other terriers were gaining fame in the showring. In 1937 it was recognized by the Irish Kennel Club, on St. Patrick's Day no less. And on St. Patrick's Day, 1962, the Soft-Coated Wheaten Terrier Club of America was founded in Brooklyn.

Height at shoulder: Males and females: 18 to 19 inches

Weight: Males and females: 35 to 45 pounds

Grooming: The Wheaten's coat is unusual for a terrier. It is fairly long, soft, and wavy. There is very little shedding, but daily brushing is important to keep the fur from matting.

Soft-Coated Wheaten Terrier

Cost: Expensive

Capabilities: This dog is apparently a terrier of all trades. Watchdog is at the top of the list, followed by hunting, herding, and then guarding. They do guard but they are better watchdogs.

Training tip: Wheatens are somewhat easier to train than other terriers. They are willing to please and are very bright. Don't let them go without obedience training, though. That terrier stubbornness will surface.

Housebreaking: No problem

Aesthetic quality: Alert, beige terrier with long, fluffy fur on his face

Personality: The Wheaten is an even-tempered animal. He remains gentle in spite of his fairly high activity level, indoors and out, so he is wonderful for younger children even though many other terriers are not. As long as he gets enough exercise, he does well in the city.

WEST HIGHLAND WHITE TERRIER

Origin: Westies go back at least to the middle of the nineteenth century in Scotland. They come from the common terrier stock of Scotland that gave us the Cairn, the Scottie, and the Dandie Dinmont. The all-white Westie was often referred to as a Reseneath or Poltalloch Terrier after the estates of their breeders. Colonel Malcolm of Poltalloch had the name officially changed to West Highland White Terrier in the first decade of the twentieth century. The white coat was valued because it made the dog much easier to see when hunting. Darker, earth-colored dogs could sometimes be mistaken for the vermin they were chasing, leading to tragic accidents.

Height at shoulder: Males: 11 inches; females: 10 inches

Weight: Males: 17 to 20 pounds; females: 15 to 18 pounds

West Highland White Terrier

Grooming: Believe it or not, that sparkling white coat is easy to keep. Too much bathing makes the coat more difficult to care for. Dry shampoo and regular brushing keep the natural oils distributed throughout the coat and do more to keep the white color clean than soap does. Westies do not shed very much, but they have the hard terrier outercoat and the soft undercoat that needs plucking when it loosens. Just gently pull the clumps of loose undercoat with the thumb and forefinger. This procedure may take a little practice.

Cost: Moderate

Capabilities: A Westie can serve as watchdog, hunter, or entertainment director. They are not good guard dogs. Not only are they too small, the West Highland White basically likes company and visitors and, though assertive, he is not an aggressive dog.

Training tip: Unlike some other terriers, Westies are not stubborn. Thus, training is a reasonably simple, straightforward affair. These are very bright dogs. Just follow a basic training course.

Housebreaking: This breed is easy to housebreak.

Aesthetic quality: Alert, perky, and white

Personality: Happy, active, sociable Highlanders enjoy life as long as they are loved, and who could not love them? Some Westies could be too impatient for a toddler or very young child. Like most terriers, a Westie will only put up with so much. But older children and Westies are a perfect combination. This breed is very active indoors and needs to play a lot. They are very active outdoors, as well. However, they make wonderful apartment dogs because they do not need an enormous amount of space for all that activity.

TOYS

ENGLISH TOY SPANIEL

Origin: Spaniel means "from Spain," and the English Toy Spaniel does have Spanish origins. However, this spaniel has a deep break in the line of the nose that suggests a pushed-up nose like the Pug or the Pekingese. This feature was probably developed in China or Japan. There is evidence of English Toy Spaniels coming from Japan to England in 1613. These luxurious little dogs come in four coat colors: King Charles (black with mahogany-tan markings on the face, chest, and legs); Prince Charles (white with black-and-tan patches); Ruby (solid chestnut red); and Blenheim (red and white).

Height at shoulder: Males and females: 9 to 10 inches

English Toy Spaniel

Weight: Males and females: 9 to 12 pounds

Grooming: There is some shedding with this breed, but not much. Regular brushing keeps the coat from matting.

Cost: Moderate

Capabilities: Companionship

Training tip: Like other spaniels, these toys are responsive and willing to please.

Housebreaking: Most members of this breed housebreak easily.

Aesthetic quality: Elegant, cheerful, pug-nosed

Personality: English Toys are charming in every way. They make perfect apartment dogs because they require very little outdoor exercise and are calm indoors. This is the only really small breed recommended, and unfortunately it is very rare. Younger children would be too rough for this dog, as would very energetic older ones.

PUG

Origin: The Chinese are usually given credit for developing dogs with pushed-in noses. They probably developed the ancient Pug. The breed has a long and varied history. There is evidence of the Pug in ancient Tibetan monasteries. The Pug also accompanied William, Prince of Orange, in sixteenth-century France, as well as Napoleon and Josephine in eighteenth-century France. They are called Pugs because of their similarity to marmosets, South and Central American monkeys which were called Pugs in the early eighteenth century. Throughout its long, illustrious history, the Pug has served strictly as a love object. These are very affectionate little toy dogs.

Height at shoulder: Males and females: 10 to 12 inches

Weight: Males and females: 14 to 18 pounds

Pug

Grooming: There is some shedding but the coat is short. Occasional brushing is good. The Pug is very easy to care for.

Cost: Moderate

Capabilities: Companionship

Training tip: Pugs can be stubborn. Be gentle and patient and don't give too many corrections. Because of their wheezy breathing, they can't take hard tugs and pulling on the leash.

Housebreaking: There should be no problems.

Aesthetic quality: Worried little tough guy

Personality: Bright, affectionate, easygoing Pugs are ideal pets for small apartments. They are not very active and do not need much exercise. Considerate school-age children are perfect with Pugs. Toddlers and rambunctious children of any age could be too rough for the dog. A Pug is loving and gentle with a child of any age. He is one of the sturdiest of the toy breeds, but he should always be treated with respect. They are often seen in pairs (a "brace").

NONSPORTING DOGS

BICHON FRISE

Origin: Bichon-type dogs lived in the Dark Ages throughout the Mediterranean region. They thrived during the
Renaissance in Spain, France, and Italy. For hundreds of
years they were kept as pets. No hunting or herding for
the Bichon. Their job is to entertain and to provide
unending love and devotion. They are experts. After

Bichon Frise

such a long history in Europe, they made the trip to the
United States in the 1950s and were accepted by the
American Kennel Club in the 1970s.

Height at shoulder: Males and females: 8 to 12 inches
Weight: Males: 14 to 20 pounds; females: 11 to 18 pounds
Grooming: This abundant, curly white coat almost never

sheds. However, extensive brushing is involved and regular visits to a professional groomer are required for trimming.

Cost: Expensive

Capabilities: Companionship is their principal talent, though they sometimes serve as watchdogs.

Training tip: Training should be easy. They are very responsive.

Housebreaking: Be patient and diligent with regard to the schedule. After perfection seems to be reached, there could be lapses. Therefore, never give up that rigid schedule.

Aesthetic quality: Fluffy, little white ball

Personality: The Bichon is so happy and sweet natured, busy and active, that it is extremely easy to live with, especially in an apartment. Although very active indoors, it needs comparatively little outdoor exercise. They are really the size of a large toy dog, so they can't withstand rough treatment from young or active children.

BOSTON TERRIER

Origin: Born and bred in Boston in the 1870s from the mating of an English Bulldog and a white English Terrier, Boston Terriers serve the sole purpose of giving and receiving affection. They always seem to have a smile on their wide little faces.

Height at shoulder: Males and females: 15 to 16 inches

Weight: Males and females: *lightweight*: under 15 pounds; *middleweight*: 15 to 20 pounds; *heavyweight*: 20 to 25 pounds

Grooming: There is some shedding, but the coat is short. Occasional brushing is a good idea. The Boston Terrier is very easy to care for.

Boston Terrier

Cost: Moderate

Capabilities: Companionship is their primary function, but they do make good watchdogs.

Training tip: There is the stubborn terrier streak here, so be patient. Expect a Boston to be responsive, particularly when the training is consistent and firm and the praise is exuberant.

Housebreaking: Include as many walks as possible in the housebreaking schedule and don't be surprised when mistakes happen. Bostons are sensitive to punishment, so simply admonish when necessary and praise lavishly when appropriate.

Aesthetic quality: Round-eyed, round-bodied, and wise

Personality: Bostons are easy to love and live with. They make wonderful city dogs because they need minimal outdoor exercise even though they are somewhat active indoors. They are not much bigger than some of the toy breeds, so some caution should govern how the children play with them. Still, Bostons can have a great time with children of all ages.

BULLDOG

Origin: This affectionate homebody was originally bred to attack bulls for sport. When bullbaiting was abolished in England in 1835, the Bulldog nearly vanished. The few people still interested in the breed for its own sake created the Bulldog we know today. The courage remains but the fighting instinct has been deliberately bred out.

Height at shoulder: Males: 15 to 16 inches; females: 14 to 15 inches

Weight: Males: 50 pounds; females: 40 pounds

Bulldog

Grooming: There is some shedding but the coat is short. Occasional brushing is good. Bulldogs do need their mouths wiped at times each day.

Cost: Expensive

Capabilities: This is a superb guard dog. He is gentle and does not become aggressive until absolutely necessary. He doesn't bark much, so as a watchdog he isn't very effective.

Training tip: When training is begun early, Bulldogs are very responsive. If too much time goes by, a stubbornness could set in.

Housebreaking: No problem

Aesthetic quality: A wheezing, snoring, drooling, magnificent animal

Personality: These legendary tough guys need and give loyalty and affection. Bulldogs only live up to their ferocious looks after extreme provocation. Any space, any place is fine since they need minimal exercise. Bulldogs love everyone in the family, including the cat. They are particularly strong and patient, which is a good combination for toddlers. They are poor at jogging and romping, which could be a drawback for an active teenager.

DALMATIAN

Origin: Dalmatians are named for Dalmatia, a region of the Balkan Peninsula on the Adriatic, where they have lived for at least two hundred years. But the people of many countries claim the Dalmatian as part of their history and culture. His service in firehouses is legendary, but then so is his service as a "coach dog," which he is sometimes called. The English have called him the "Spotted Dick" and the "Plum Pudding Dog." The Dalmatian also has a long association with Gypsies.

Dalmatian

Clearly this is an adaptable, popular dog.

Height at shoulder: Males and females: 19 to 23 inches

Weight: Males and females: 50 to 65 pounds

Grooming: Dalmatians do shed, but their coats are very short and flat. Regular brushing helps.

Cost: Moderate

Capabilities: These dogs have served their many admirers in many ways. They can haul loads, herd flocks, or serve in the military as sentry dogs. They can hunt and retrieve fowl, follow a scent, or even hunt large game. They have performed in circus acts and been trained for guard work. They work well with horses and have tremendous endurance.

Training tip: Dalmatians require a calm, firm, patient trainer. Because the dog can be excitable, praise him quietly and gently. Dalmatians are intrinsically stubborn, but their desire to please their owners is so great that they overcome that innate resistance.

Housebreaking: This breed housebreaks with no problems.

Aesthetic quality: Black spots on a large, white dog

Personality: These active, strong dogs need a lot of exercise inside and out. Active children with a love for running and romping would be a good match for a Dalmatian. This dog is probably too big and active for very young children. When buying a Dalmatian for children, be sure to go to a reputable breeder who can show you good, steady bloodlines. The city is a viable option if the dog is exercised faithfully.

KEESHOND

Origin: For several hundred years the pet dog in Holland has been the Keeshond. It was named for Kees de Gyselaer of Dordrecht, the political opponent of the prince of Orange in the latter part of the eighteenth century. Before that it had simply been "the people's dog." The prince of Orange won the contest, established his political party as the dominant one, causing the Keeshond to decrease in number until 1920, when the baroness van Hardenbroek of Holland became his patroness. Keeshonds now enjoy international acceptance.

Height at shoulder: Males: 18 inches; females: 17 inches

Weight: Males: 40 pounds; females: 35 pounds

Grooming: The harsh outercoat and the heavy undercoat shed all year long. In late spring and early fall the shedding is heavier to prepare for the new season. Frequent brushing helps. Frequent baths don't.

Cost: Moderate

Keeshond

Capabilities: These are principally companion dogs, though they can perform as excellent watchdogs.

Training tip: Keeshonds are responsive and easily trained.

Housebreaking: No problem

Aesthetic quality: Fox-like face with heavy coat of northern dogs

Personality: These easy-to-live-with dogs can adapt to all lifestyles. They get along well with children of all ages and they can handle city life quite nicely for an active dog. A reasonable amount of exercise is good for them.

POODLE (MINIATURE AND STANDARD)

Origin: The name *Poodle* comes from the German *pudeln* (to splash in water) and the Poodle itself evidently comes from Germany, though its history goes so far back that there are no conclusive records. The name "French Poodle" is a misnomer, although the French do indeed love the dog. They call it the *Caniche* (duck dog). The breed began as a Standard Poodle, a water retriever of remarkable skill and intelligence. They are also famous as dancers and tricksters. The Poodle is always clipped, whether in a natural, even, sporting clip or one of the fancy show clips, because his fur grows like human hair; it does not stop. Unclipped, the Poodle's coat is very difficult to manage. Only the Miniature and Standard varieties are recommended for children.

Miniature Poodle

Miniature Poodle

Height at shoulder: Males and females: over 10 inches to 15 inches

Weight: Males: 15 to 20 pounds; females: 12 to 18 pounds

Standard Poodle

Height at shoulder: Males and females: over 15 inches
Weight: Males: 45 to 60 pounds; females: 40 to 50 pounds

Standard Poodle

Grooming: There is almost no shedding, but the Poodle needs regular brushing and regular trips to a professional groomer for clipping.

Cost: Moderate

Capabilities: Some Standard Poodles can be trained for guard work. All Poodles are good watchdogs. Most of them love to swim. Standards can be trained to hunt fowl, and Miniatures can be trained to do all kinds of tricks.

Training tip: Poodles are extremely bright and responsive. They can learn just about anything they are taught.

Housebreaking: No problem

Aesthetic quality: Sculpted, cosmopolitan sophisticate or rugged sporting dog depending on coat clip and lifestyle

Personality: Poodles win all popularity contests because they are extremely intelligent, cooperative, and sensitive to their owner's needs. Only a poorly bred Poodle shows any negative qualities. Miniatures are more active than Standards, and thus need just as much living space. Both varieties need daily outdoor exercise. Standards are large, active dogs that could overwhelm toddlers. Now and then a Miniature is too high-strung for a very small child. Both sizes are wonderful with older children.

Bearded Collie

HERDING DOGS

BEARDED COLLIE

Origin: These herding dogs from southern Scotland were painted by Gainsborough in 1771 in a portrait of the duke of Buccleuch. They seem to be descended from the Magyar Komondor of central Europe. The Bearded Collie offers Americans an opportunity to own a very "new" old breed that was not bred in America until the 1960s.

Height at shoulder: Males: 21 to 22 inches; females: 20 to 21 inches

Weight: Males: 45 to 55 pounds; females: 40 to 50 pounds

Grooming: Considering this breed's double coat (hard outercoat and downy undercoat), there is not as much shedding as one might think. But regular, thorough brushing is required.

Cost: Expensive

Capabilities: Bearded Collies will herd sheep, cattle, and children. They are good watchdogs but not guard dogs.

Training tip: These are responsive, easily trained dogs.

Housebreaking: There are no particular problems.

Aesthetic quality: Fluffy, medium-sized sheep dog

Personality: Bearded Collies are splendid with all children but they do tend to think they are in charge. A medium to large apartment makes city life a reasonable choice since exercise is important to this dog both indoors and outdoors.

BOUVIER DES FLANDRES

Origin: The Bouvier served as a cattle drover for the farmers and butchers of northern France in the late nineteenth century. Many were lost when northern

France was captured in World War I, but some survived through working in the French military.

Height at shoulder: Males: 24½ to 27½ inches; females: 23½ to 26½ inches

Weight: Males: 85 to 100 pounds; females: 75 to 90 pounds

Bouvier des Flandres

Grooming: Like all herding dogs, the Bouvier has a long, hard outercoat over a shorter, downy undercoat. Shedding continues all year-round but is heaviest during late spring and early fall when the coat adjusts to the new season. The Bouvier needs regular, thorough brushing. They also require periodic visits to a professional groomer for trimming.

Cost: Expensive

Capabilities: Bouviers are wonderful, effective guard dogs, watchdogs, and drovers.

Training tip: Bouvier owners are fortunate that dogs of this breed train well because they are large, powerful dogs that must not go untrained. They are bright and willing to please, so all Bouviers should be well behaved.

Housebreaking: No problem

Aesthetic quality: Large, woolly, dominant animal

Personality: This large, exuberant dog loves and needs to run. He is probably best for older children because he is so energetic; however, he settles down once he is inside. Apartment living is possible if the apartment is large enough and the dog can receive daily outdoor exercise. Bouviers are happiest when they are with their own families, especially the children.

COLLIE (SMOOTH AND ROUGH)

Origin: The name *Collie* comes from the English word *colly,* meaning "black." The original Collies before the nineteenth century were either black or black and white. The famous sable and white coloring was developed around 1870. During this time the tricolor coat and the blue merle (blue-gray with splotches of black) were also developed. Both the well-known Rough Collie and the lesser known Smooth Collie come with a variety of coats; sable and white; tricolor; blue merle; and white (which also has some sable, tricolor, or blue-merle markings). Thanks to Lassie, everyone knows that Collies are sheepherders from the Scottish Highlands.

Height at shoulder: Males: 24 to 26 inches; females: 22 to 24 inches

Weight: Males: 60 to 75 pounds; females: 40 to 65 pounds

Collie

Grooming: Both the Smooth and the Rough Collies have double coats. The outercoat on the Rough variety is long and stands out from the body to give that typical "Lassie" look. The outercoat on the Smooth variety is short and lies flat to the body. Both varieties have a short, dense undercoat. Both varieties shed, especially in the late spring and early fall when the coat adjusts to the new season. Regular brushing is essential, but Collies do not need much clipping or trimming. Professional grooming is unnecessary unless the rough coat has been neglected for a period of time.

Cost: Expensive

Capabilities: Herding, protective instincts make the Collie an excellent watchdog. In addition, many Collies can be trained to guard.

Training tip: All Collies tend to be very bright and responsive and easily trained. Begin training early to avoid a stubbornness that can develop in an untrained dog. Avoid punishing a Collie: they are sensitive and respond poorly to such treatment. Hitting them can make them aggressive.

Housebreaking: There should be no problem.

Aesthetic quality: Graceful, warm, dignified beauty

Personality: These are affectionate, intelligent, loyal dogs who take their family responsibilities seriously. They treat young children and toddlers like spring lambs needing a lot of care. If given enough outdoor exercise, they are not too active inside and adjust well to apartment living. Be sure to get a well-bred puppy for children.

GERMAN SHEPHERD DOG

Origin: At the end of the nineteenth century, a number of different German herding dogs were bred together for their intelligence and herding ability. Conformation was considered only with regard to the dog's work performance. The result was the German Shepherd Dog which lives to serve its human master. The German

German Shephard Dog

Shepherd can be taught any number of tasks and is famous for its service to blind persons, the police, and the military. Nearly forgotten is its talent as a herder.

Height at shoulder: Males: 24 to 26 inches; females: 22 to 24 inches

Weight: Males: 75 to 85 pounds; females: 60 to 70 pounds

Grooming: The Shepherd has the herding dog's hard outercoat and downy undercoat that shed all year-round, but particularly in the late spring and early fall. They need a lot of brushing but no professional care.

Cost: Expensive

Capabilities: This breed's abilities are its reason for being. They are superior guard dogs and watchdogs and wonderful, devoted companions. They even have good noses and are often trained to detect bombs or narcotics.

Training tip: The German Shepherd Dog is eminently trainable. The dog is so intelligent that punishment is offensive. These are very bright, sensitive dogs. Abuse is counterproductive. Simply correct unwanted behavior with a dominant demeanor, and consistently praise achievement.

Housebreaking: No special problems

Aesthetic quality: The classic image of the faithful and noble friend

Personality: Shepherds need the respect and love of their families above all else. The children are the dog's self-determined responsibility. All ages and types of children will be well cared for. Exercise is important. Shepherds are powerful, active dogs and will be active indoors even with a daily outdoor exercise period. Thus, a small apartment is not appropriate, although they will adjust to any environment if necessary. The reports of aggressive behavior attributed to these dogs generally refer only to a poorly bred or mistreated animal, so select a well-bred puppy from a responsible breeder.

PEMBROKE WELSH CORGI

Origin: Henry I brought Flemish weavers to England in 1107. They made their home in southwestern Wales. With them came their dogs, descendants of northern Spitz-types. These dogs are known today as Pembroke Welsh Corgis. The Cardigan Welsh Corgi is descended from the Dachshund, but because the two Corgis were interbred in the nineteenth century they are now very similar in appearance. Pembrokes are the Corgis with pointed ears and almost no tail. The Cardigans have more-rounded ears and long tails. For hundreds of years Corgis served their masters by nipping the heels of neighbors' cattle to keep them off their grazing land.

Pembroke Welsh Corgi

Height at shoulder: Males and females: 10 to 12 inches
Weight: Males: 27 to 30 pounds; females: 25 to 28 pounds
Grooming: The medium-length outercoat and downy undercoat shed all year long, especially in the late spring and early fall. Regular brushing is helpful.

Cost: Moderate

Capabilities: Corgis are natural guard dogs and watch-dogs.

Training tip: They are very bright and learn easily.

Housebreaking: There should be no problems.

Aesthetic quality: Fox-like head on long, low, tailless body

Personality: The Pembroke is a bit more outgoing than the Cardigan and probably relates to children more easily, although they both like children. Older children usually get along with this breed better than younger children. The dominance of older children is more acceptable to these decision-making cattle dogs. These dogs are very active indoors. Apartments, houses, or acres of countryside are all fine given their moderate need for exercise.

SHETLAND SHEEPDOG

Origin: The Sheltie descends from the same Scottish sheepherders as the modern Collie. But the Sheltie is a much smaller version. The people of the Shetland Islands, off the northern coast of Scotland, allowed the Sheltie to develop quietly. The breed went unnoticed by the rest of the world until the beginning of the twentieth century.

Height at shoulder: Males and females: 13 to 16 inches

Weight: Males and females: 15 to 20 pounds

Grooming: The long outercoat and downy undercoat shed all year long. Shedding is especially heavy during the late spring and early fall when the coat adjusts to the change in temperature. Regular brushing is essential.

Cost: Moderate

Capabilities: Warning strangers and sounding the alarm

Shetland Sheepdog

to strange noises are well within the Sheltie's talents, but guarding is not.

Training tip: This is a sensitive breed and as such does very poorly when punished or treated harshly. They become shy if mistreated. Train them easily and gently to maintain their sweet temperaments.

Housebreaking: There should be no problems.

Aesthetic quality: Miniature version of Lassie

Personality: Shelties need older, more thoughtful children who will not roughhouse with them. Even though they are relatively small, they like outdoor exercise and remain moderately active indoors. This breed is a good choice for apartment dwellers if the dog is introduced to the environment early. An older dog seeing buses and hearing taxis for the first time may be frightened.

MISCELLANEOUS CLASS

Cavalier King Charles Spaniel

CAVALIER KING CHARLES SPANIEL

Origin: European palaces and portraits of the sixteenth, seventeenth, and eighteenth centuries were filled with Toy Spaniels. Many spaniels from those centuries looked just like the Cavalier of today. In the nineteenth century, the Toy Spaniel was bred for a more-domed head and a pushed-up nose. This breed is known as the English Toy Spaniel. Interest returned to the original dog when an American, Roswell Eldridge, offered a prize at the Crofts Show in England in 1926, 1927, and 1928 for the dog most like the old "nosey" type. The Cavalier King Charles Spaniel was developed from the older "nosey"-type dogs and from some larger spaniels. The Cavalier has the ability to scent and flush game in the field if trained for it. It can also serve as the perfect house pet, making for a rare combination in a small dog. The Cavalier comes in the same colors as the English Toy Spaniel. Breeders of the Cavalier in this country are very conservative about the expansion of the breed. Cavaliers do not yet compete in a regular class in the American Kennel Club; they remain in the Miscellaneous Class.

Height at shoulder: Males and females: 12 to 13 inches

Weight: Males and females: 12 to 18 pounds

Grooming: There is a little shedding. Regular brushing keeps the fur from matting.

Cost: Very expensive

Capabilities: Companionship, or flushing fowl for the hunter

Training tip: They are very responsive and eager to please.

Housebreaking: Frequent walks, consistent schedules, and patience will help. The Cavalier sometimes has difficulty with housebreaking.

Aesthetic quality: Elegant, classic, cheerful

Personality: Cavaliers are loving and playful with all children. They have the spaniel talent of being able to relate to every member of a large family as though each person were the favorite. The Cavalier is not as delicate as the English Toy Spaniel, but young children and toddlers should be supervised. This breed is a delight to live with and extremely easy to care for. They are reasonably active indoors but do not need extensive outdoor exercise, which makes them wonderful city dogs.

IDEAL MUTT

The earliest wolves to leave the prehistoric forests and join human campfires were the first mutts. It is with some justification that humans conjure up romantic visions of mutts. Part wolf, part coyote, part fox, the first mutts were the forerunners of today's purebreds. More people live with mutts than with any other dog.

The principal difference between purebreds and mutts is the predictability of the look, type, and, to a lesser degree, behavior of the purebred. Mutts should not be confused with mixed breeds. A part-Poodle, part-spaniel is fairly obvious. The so-called Cock-A-Poo is thought of by many pet owners as an actual breed. If the dog's parents are known but of different breeds, you can at least guess what the puppies will be like. Not so with a mutt. Mutt puppies are mystery dogs. This type of dog is an adventure in genetics.

Mutts, or mongrels, generally fall into one of several categories of physical appearance. The most basic mutt type is a small to medium coyote-fox-looking dog. The fur is most often red to brown with a white blaze on the chest. Next is the police dog look. These are medium to large dogs most often seen with a gray to black coat. They resemble German Shepherd Dogs. A fairly common mutt type is the medium-sized Spitz look. They are most often white or white and black with a furry mane and a curly tail. They derive from the northern or sled dog types. There is also a spaniel-looking mutt and a setter-looking mutt. Among the most popular mutt types are those that are obviously from terrier breeds. The breed most common in films, TV, and commercials is a medium to large, shaggy terrier type that resembles an Old English Sheepdog, an Otter Hound, or a Bearded Collie. Then there are the small to medium wire-haired terrier types. This type is very popular. One often finds a small to medium, smooth-coated terrier-hound with white fur and black patches. A toy-sized mutt is a rarity, but they are around. The most commonly admired mutt is the medium-sized dog that looks like a yellow Labrador Retriever. It always has a wise, engaging look in its eyes.

Ideal mutt

Generally speaking, if the mongrel puppy is large for his age and has big paws, he will grow into a large animal that could be too much dog for small children. Another clue to look for is how the puppy behaves in his litter or in his cage. Just as when choosing a purebred puppy, pick the one who comes to the front and wants you to take him home. He will probably enjoy the children more and be a little easier to train. A dog's temperament is far more important than its look. You would be surprised how quickly one comes to love a sweet-natured, intelligent dog that may at first seem something of an eyesore. It is a universal truth that a dog's beauty, like a child's, is present from a source deep within and hidden from the uncaring.

—3—

UNDERSTANDING
YOUR DOG

To the family trying to cope with a dog that eats furniture, dumps on the bed, barks at the landlord, and lifts its leg on shopping carts loaded with bags of food, I offer my sympathy. More than that, I offer this chapter. Believe it or not, a great deal can be accomplished with a dog when you understand why he does what he does. Knowing the basics of dog behavior helps you decide how to solve the dog's living problems. You see, you only have three ways to proceed to make a dog more livable. One, you can have the dog obedience trained (either by a trainer or a member of the family). Two, you can manipulate the dog's living conditions to accommodate his particular difficulties as well as your sensibilities. Three, you can try some type of behavior modification as practiced by dog behaviorists. Actually, all dog training can be regarded as a form of behavior modification.

After living with a dog for several months, many will proclaim that he is neurotic. When they leave the house he pees on the carpet and leaves a mess someplace. This behavior is always interpreted as the dog's spite in return for having been left alone. But is a dog neurotic or spiteful if, when confronted with a set of circumstances that parallels a similar situation in the wild, he obeys every impulse that is true to his nature? It is unreasonable to expect a dog to behave differently just because the demands of domesticity clash with natural canine behavior.

Is your dog unable to develop and sustain a meaningful relationship? Does she scramble for cheap thrills in order to hide from reality? These are human problems, as are other aspects of neurotic behavior. Dog owners often seem to receive undue pleasure by announcing that their pets are neurotic. Pet owners need to understand the difference between "normal" and "problem" behavior and forget the word "neurotic" when it comes to animals.

If your dog were to chain-smoke and pace all night, it would probably be neurotic. But if it did that, it would not be a dog. On the other hand, if it quakes with fear during a thunderstorm it definitely has a dog problem. It is possible to take a specific fear, a phobia if you will, and generalize it to a point where the dog is irrationally frightened of all manner of things that are not really threatening, such as unknown people and moving cars.

The following actions represent the most common forms of canine problem behavior: housebreaking failures; aggressiveness (threatening, biting, attacking); failure to obey humans; nervousness (barking, digging, chewing, jumping, or running away); fear responses (cringing, hiding, shaking, nipping, wetting, chewing, barking); phobias (fear of confinement, isolation, thunder, strangers, outdoors, mechanical noises, etc.). I'm sure you can add more to this list.

In many cases, something in the dog's living environment is disturbing the animal. These disturbances can range from the ringing of the telephone to something a child is doing. There are certain aspects of childhood that could be disturbing or frightening to a dog. As a child gets older it grows bigger. For some dogs a growing child can threaten the dog's position of dominance in the family, or pack, structure. This is the type of situation where a knowledge of basic dog behavior will help.

Obviously, abusive or inhumane treatment will alter a dog's behavior. A death in the family, a divorce, a child going off to school for the first time, and boarding the dog are events that can almost guarantee a response in the dog's nervous system. Boredom and loneliness, however, are the two greatest factors in creating problem behavior in dogs. Also, aggressive dogs may be expressing a medical problem or the result of early abuse. The same can be true of a shy or nervous dog. Moreover, a dog may inherit these qualities from its parents, grandparents, great-grandparents, etc., or follow its breed characteristics to the extreme due to poor breeding. Such problems are often solved by firmly establishing a subordinate attitude in the dog and a dominant attitude in the human. Dog trainers are extremely helpful in effecting this change. It has been my experience that few behavioral problems are unsolvable. I recommend a professional dog trainer or a do-it-yourself dog training book. If the problem persists, then consult with one of the new breed of animal psychologists and pass the Kleenex. Actually, the nature of many problems and their solutions become clear when you understand basic dog behavior.

BASIC DOG BEHAVIOR

Dogs behave in certain predictable ways given the influence of external factors such as the behavior of the dog's mother, litter mates, or human beings. What puppies and human babies have in common is the influence of early experiences which profoundly affect later behavior. Dog behavior is determined by genetics and is also shaped by environmental influences. These factors are filtered through the sensory mechanisms (eyes, ears, nose, etc.) acting upon the nervous system. There are known factors in basic dog behavior that are present at birth in all dogs. In other words, there is such a thing as *classic dog behavior*. An understanding of this behavior can help one to measure the behavior of all dogs.

First, it is important to realize that the dog, with all its variety of breeds, is a descendant of the wolf. From the Chihuahua to the Saint Bernard, all dogs are related to each other and share the wolf as their common ancestor and present-day cousin. Even wolves vary in size, color, and characteristics. The great physical and behavioral differences among dog breeds are the result of twelve thousand years of domestication plus the genetic tinkering of humans involved in breeding them. Still, it is a safe statement, if not altogether proven, that dog behavior is a modified form of wolf behavior. A great deal is known about wolf behavior and has been successfully applied to the study of dogs.

The most important aspects of classic dog (or wolf) behavior are:

1. They live in groups known as *packs*.
2. They form social attachments.
3. They require a leader.
4. They claim territory.
5. They survive by hunting prey animals for food.
6. They mate and produce offspring.

The Pack

Dogs were born to live in social units referred to as *packs*. The pack works as a team to hunt for food, defend its territory, and accomplish the various tasks connected with survival. Pack behavior reflects the dog's need to be with other creatures. When they live as pets, this need is transferred to humans, provided that the dogs were socialized with people during the seventh or eighth week of life. This early socialization period is critical. The human family is then viewed as a substitute pack by the dog, even if there is only one person in the family. This fact explains why dogs are constant and loyal companions.

There can be no doubt that the purpose of the dog or wolf pack is to enable this relatively small animal to hunt for large game. As a pack they have the ability to track and attack animals such as moose, elk, deer, wild sheep, and reindeer. One dog or wolf alone could never tackle animals of this size. Smaller animals are brought down by one wolf.

As wolves become older, at about two years of age, they become less and less tolerant of newcomers joining the pack. This wariness often leads to dangerous fights, sometimes to the death. Although this behavior does not exist as such among dogs, there are traces of it in some of the more territorial breeds, especially among very aggressive males. Among dogs, many of the working and herding breeds are more territorial and tend to protect their families, especially the children. Visitors, even young ones, must be introduced to this type of dog lest they be met with suspicion and/or hostile behavior.

There are few mammals that live in so highly established a group as do wolves and wild dogs. The dog, it would seem, is a domesticated version of these wild animals. As such, it fits neatly into the group-oriented structure of human society. Not even the domestic cat can blend in so well with the lifestyle and behavior engendered by human social patterns. Pet cats live somewhat apart from humans, while dogs participate in every imaginable activity if allowed. Humans and dogs have much in common.

Social Attachments

Within a pack society, social attachments develop as a matter of course. It is the dogs' need to be with other creatures while enjoying all the contact involved that makes them so lovable and suitable as home companions. All members of the pack remain secure so long as challenges are not made to the established order of rank, privilege, and performance. Very meaningful relationships can develop because of a dog's need for a pack structure and a human's desire for emotional contact that is unchallenged and unqualified. All humans, adults as well as children, share with dogs a natural curiosity and dependency, each giving something, each getting something.

The pack is a social unit that stems from pairing, where one female and one male stay together for the purpose of sharing the tasks associated with survival and procreation. This behavior still exists in the dog's other cousins, the fox and the coyote. The pack is a kind of economic and social system much like those that exist in human societies to hold groups of related families together with a loose but efficient system. A "pair bond" develops between males and females, making it possible for litters of cubs or pups to be born and reared. New packs are formed when males and females pair off to mate, whelp young, and establish their own lives independent of their parents. We could almost be discussing postadolescent humans. The domestic dog has as great a need for social attachments as its wild cousin, the wolf. If humans become involved with puppies at the critical period, the social attachments become directed toward humans as well as toward dogs. That is the ideal situation in which to raise a pet dog.

Need for a Leader

The dog or wolf pack requires a minimum of conflict within its ranks in order to function well. This stability is achieved through an inherited factor of dominant or subordinate tendencies that is "programmed" into every wolf or dog. A "leader of the pack" always emerges, along with other dominant and subordinate pack members who manage to sort themselves out into some kind of order according to rank. This hierarchy helps dogs or wolves living in the wild to survive. The need for leadership is primary if the group is to survive.

When a dog is introduced into a human household, it will still assume that it is a member of a pack. If you carefully observe the behavior of the most timid or aggressive house dog you will see a dog that needs to know its place within the pack. Every dog requires that someone assume a leadership position. Your family pet will accept the position of command if no one else will. Dogs are insecure without a leader and have been known to take charge of complex households. Conversely, they accept leadership from those with dominant personalities or from those who behave with some degree of authority. Once you assume the position of leader, your dog will accept it for the rest of his life. Many people, especially children, have difficulty being dominant over the family dog. There are many factors at work. These factors include the individual human's personality, age, and experience. The dog's size, temperament, breed, and early influences also play an important role. Once you begin to learn about dog behavior, you will come to understand that your dog's training will partly be concerned with establishing its place within the pack.

In the wild, dominant dogs or wolves have first access to food, shelter, and mates. The original pair that forms a new pack are its leaders (for a while) and they are referred to by researchers as *alpha males* or *alpha females*. The position of rank begins to form early in puppyhood and can be witnessed during the latter stages of breast-feeding and during episodes of puppy play fighting. If the youngsters remain with the litter beyond sixteen weeks, one can observe totally dominant and totally subordinate dogs. From twelve to sixteen weeks of life in the pack or litter, puppies engage in hostile encounters involving aggressive displays and combats. Fights ensue but end quickly, with the establishment of rank being the result.

In the center of every pack is the alpha male. This dog behaves with a brooding dominance that is feared and respected by all. All members of the pack look to him for the first reaction to anything out of the ordinary, such as the invasion of their territory by an intruder. The alpha male usually leads all chases and accepts nothing less than total submission on issues involving hunting, feeding, and mating. In a sense, the alpha male is an absolute autocrat. When a wolf asserts its dominance over another wolf he stands straight, with his ears erect and his tail in a horizontal position. The teeth are bared with a frightening upward wrinkling of the lips, and a deep growl is given. The lesser wolf assumes a lower posture and flattens its ears as its tail lowers between its legs. The "top dog" is established when the dominant animal stands over the submissive one with his head over the other's neck and abdomen. This ritualized behavior helps to avoid many fights and minimizes disruptions of pack routine.

In the home, domestic dogs will forever attempt to display dominant behavior unless taught otherwise. With a puppy of normal temperament, there will be at least one "showdown" situation where a member of the family will either assert dominance and establish the dog's subordinate rank, or, be ruled over or even bullied by the family pet. The opportunity most often presents itself during the first or second session of obedience, training when the dog insists on walking in one direction while the human insists on another. With a firm, intelligent use of the leash, without abuse, the person wins out and sends a loud and clear message to the dog. A dominant manner on the part of the human will effectively reinforce the newly established order in the mind of the young dog.

Territory

Dogs, like other meat eaters, instinctively require an area for hunting and, within that area, a place for sleeping. These activity zones are referred to as *territory*. The hunting area is the dog or wolf pack's *range*, which is shared with other animals. The sleeping area is the *den*, which is also used as a nest for whelping newborns and as a lair for the youngsters' safety. A den may be a cave, a tunnel, or even a hollow log.

Although dogs and wolves regard their hunting range as territory, they will seldom fight to defend it. However, the den is guarded with vigor. In our homes the dog may consider the entire house or apartment as the den, or simply his small section of it. His range may include a backyard or an entire neighborhood. It depends upon the individual dog. Certainly, a doghouse or collapsible wire crate (a form of traveling cage), or anything resembling it, is considered a den. The place where your dog rests is an element in his life that provides comfort and security. It is very important to him. Dogs feel best when they can enjoy the peace and comfort of the den.

Three important aspects of the domestic dog's behavior stem from canine territorial instincts. First, many pet dogs respond aggressively when a stranger approaches their territory. This territory could include your entire grounds or your house or simply where the dog's food bowl is placed. Aggression toward strangers will occur if the dog is dominant. Obedience training coupled with a dominant demeanor on behalf of the dog's master will help to keep aggressive behavior to a minimum. Second, all dogs *mark*, or *scent post*, their territory for the purpose of claiming it as their own. Marking is accomplished with urine and feces. Territory is sometimes marked by scratching the ground with the front paws. Dogs will try to do this on cement surfaces as well. Although no one is absolutely certain why dogs scent post, it can reasonably be assumed that they are claiming territory with their urine and/or leaving a message for other dogs. The human family should allow the dog to scent post outside the home at specific locations. Here, housebreaking is served by intelligent manipulation of the dog's instincts. Third, a den, or inner core, is required. A pet dog lacking a den can become quite emotionally stressed. This stress can easily be prevented by providing your dog with a man-made den. Consider purchasing a collapsible wire crate with a door in front, a solid floor, and a wire roof. You can make the crate quite comfortable by placing a mat or blanket on the bottom. Spread a blanket over the top to provide your dog with a tent-like privacy. The den area should belong exclusively to the dog. All dogs need to have a place where they can rest or retreat without being disturbed. It is an act of intelligence and kindness to make the dog's den area, wherever or whatever it may be, off-limits to everyone, especially children. As a child needs the refuge of his own room, so, too, does a dog.

Hunting

Although most domestic dogs no longer have to hunt to survive, some hunting behavior remains as an instinctive reaction to certain stimuli. Most hunting is a pack activity, particularly when the prey is a large animal. Hunting requires the utmost of cooperation and team effort to succeed. Wolves and wild dogs hunt in the open and rarely stalk or ambush, as do cats. The prey, if it is large, is almost always a herd animal and one that is too weak to stay with its herd. The method of hunting is to give chase through long-distance running, with one wolf attacking the prey's hindquarters as the others attack from the front.

The various hunting skills of wolves and wild dogs can be seen in individual domestic dog breeds, but in a diluted and piecemeal fashion. Each breed has been refined as a specialist rather than as an all-round general practitioner. Through selective breeding, one or more of the various hunting skills have become emphasized to the detriment of other hunting skills. For example, sheepdogs and cattle dogs have developed their herding and droving skills as an outgrowth of hunting techniques that involved moving a prey animal toward waiting members of the pack. Hunting dogs have been bred for either their sense of smell or sight to assist the human hunter. Retrievers have been bred to carry home downed birds without biting hard, thus preserving the birds as food for the human. Working breeds guard, protect, haul, or attack on command. These skills all originally contributed to the survival of a wolf or wild dog pack.

Pet owners should certainly read about the hunting skills of the dog breed they live with. Then their dog can be compared to its wild cousins and seen in a more understandable context. Clearly, then, no adult or child should behave in a manner that elicits a dog's aggressive or hunting instincts. A child darting quickly in front of a family dog is enough to set in motion deeply buried and seldom-seen reactions such as running, jumping, growling, or even attacking. The same is true of tug-of-war games with a towel or dog toy. Know how to avoid encouraging a dog's dormant instincts for aggression.

Mating and Producing Offspring

Dogs are at least twice as fertile as wolves. They are capable of mating twice a year (wolves mate once a year) and producing much larger litters of pups. The dog's capacity for mating is thought to have evolved through domesticity. Nature has provided a set of checks and balances that limits the fertility rate among wolves. Large wolf packs do not function well and have difficulty maintaining a food supply for all, given their need to live off the land. Along with the limited food supply, there is increased competition for mates, leadership, and dominance. The net result is a huge population of domestic dogs and a much smaller population of wolves. Of course, the encroachment by society upon the environment and the killing of wolves to protect herds and flocks of food animals has done more to decimate the wolf population than anything nature had planned. These facts notwithstanding, there would always have been more domestic dogs than wolves.

The sexual behavior of dogs is thought to be simply a modification of the sexual behavior of wolves. The alpha male of the pack has greater access to females in estrus (heat) than others, but not exclusive access. Other dominant males, while showing preferences for certain females, are still subject to being chosen by more dominant females and do not mate until the female has indicated her readiness.

There is little or no sexual behavior among dogs until the female enters estrus. The normal estrous period lasts twenty-one days. The first sign of estrus is a slight discharge of blood from the vagina. The female gives off an odor (imperceptible to humans) that alerts males in the vicinity. The actual period of receptivity by the female to the male dog lasts only six to twelve days. The pattern for canine copulation involves mutual investigation of the genital areas. The female moves her tail to one side while standing still. The male mounts from the rear while clasping the female with his front paws. Once the penis is inserted, the male thrusts his pelvis forward in rapid succession. The tissue within the penis becomes engorged with blood, causing it to swell. This creates a "tie" or lock that holds the two dogs together until ejaculation. While still locked together, the male dismounts and turns in the opposite direction, forcing the two dogs to stand tail-to-tail. The dogs may take several minutes before they are able to release from the "tie." It is a noisy encounter and is frightening to the uninitiated, particularly children.

A female dog takes nine weeks (sixty-three days) to whelp a litter of puppies. This length of time represents an estimate because ovulation takes place approximately seventy-two hours before the end of receptivity. It takes three weeks for the fertilized eggs to become implanted in the dog's uterus. When the puppies are born it is possible for them to be delivered up to twenty-four hours apart, although that is not common.

THE CRITICAL PERIODS OF PUPPY DEVELOPMENT

Pet dogs have much to tolerate, especially if they are going to live with children. There is one thing a dog needs if it is to survive three kids, a Frisbee, and a bag of potato chips, and that is an even, easygoing temperament. This temperament is not too difficult to find in a dog if it was *socialized* at the right time during puppyhood. A dog of good temperament is one that is adaptive to living with human beings without fear or hesitation. Unfortunately, some dogs have difficulty adjusting from life in the puppy litter to life in the human litter. These are the dogs that are more likely to be shy, timid, nervous, overly aggressive, or downright dangerous. Apart from any inherited genetic behavior and breed characteristics, such problems may stem from a lack of socializing during puppyhood.

There are specific periods of time in a puppy's life when the slightest experience has the greatest impact on future behavior. These specific times are critical periods. These critical periods last for a short time and yet have the greatest impact in determining the dog the puppy will become. Few serious breeders in this country are unaware of the techniques of socializing and its importance during the critical periods of puppyhood. I cannot urge you strongly enough to be certain that your next puppy be one that was socialized at the proper time. It can make the difference between a great dog and a so-so dog.

From Birth to the Thirteenth Day (Neonatal Period)

During this period the newborn puppy is completely dependent on its mother for everything. Its eyes and ears are closed and its ability to move about is restricted to a slow, forward motion. The nervous system is at a primitive stage of development and the pup cannot even maintain its own body temperature. The mother dog provides milk, warmth, and even the process of digestion through stimulation of the outer abdominal area with her tongue. There is no discernible learning during this period. Life for a neonatal pup consists of crawling about in search of warmth and nutrition.

The Thirteenth to the Twentieth Day
(Transitional Period)

A rapid transformation begins at this time in the puppy's life. His eyes open and he begins to walk instead of crawl. Exploration of the world beyond the mother's teat is the most noticeable change. With the further development of the motor and sensory capacities, the little dog begins to interact with its environment. The tail begins to wag and the pup tries to satisfy its own needs. At this stage it can also experience pain. At the end of this period the puppy is capable of leaving the nest for the purpose of independent urination and defecation. Also, the ears open, allowing for responses to loud noises. On the twentieth day the teeth begin to erupt from the gums. The sleeping puppy is easily distinguished from the puppy that is awake. Almost all sensory and motor abilities are in place and functioning. The dog is about to enter a period of learning about creatures other than itself.

The Third Week to the Seventh Week
(Beginning of Socialization)

It is difficult to pinpoint the exact time when one phase ends and the next begins, but the times stated are sufficiently descriptive. Because the pup's sensory and motor capacities are not yet fully developed, he is still somewhat clumsy and uncoordinated. During this period the most important development consists of the beginning of social behavior. Over the next four weeks the brain and nervous system develop to the point of adult maturity. At the same time, the puppy begins to socialize with its mother and litter mates. This canine socialization is extremely important. During this time the young dog learns to adjust to other dogs. Without the experiences of this period the dog will always be distrustful of other dogs and constantly pick fights with them as an adult.

At this time, the process of weaning away from breast milk to whole food has begun, along with more sophisticated urination and defecation behavior. The areas used for this purpose become well defined and are situated farther from the nest. A sleeping puppy can refrain from eliminating for many hours. Also, puppies are learning to holler for help when they need it. If they are separated from the mother or other litter mates, they will cause a racket. Play and play fighting with litter mates is apparent, along with intense investigatory behavior. The puppy will respond to the sight or sound of people or other animals with tail-wagging enthusiasm. Up until this period the puppies engage in independent movement. But after the fourth week they begin to follow each other around and by five weeks move together as a group. This behavior represents the beginnings of adult pack behavior.

By the seventh week, weaning is complete. The mother refuses the puppies access to her breasts and threatens them when they try to nurse. It is at this time that humans intervene and socialize the puppies. When a puppy is handled for short periods of time by humans, from the fifth week of puppyhood on, that animal grows to be highly adaptive to living with humans. However, it is extremely important that these short spans of affectionate handling be limited to only several times a day and that the dog remain with its litter for the rest of the time. This approach assures the puppy's socialization to both humans and dogs.

The Eighth Week to the Twelfth Week
(Final Phase of Socialization)

The puppy is now capable of vocalizing with greater variety and maturity. Although pups tend to cry less, when they are in strange places they will bark, which indicates an assertive attitude. Coordination is much improved and with it one sees the development of the ability to run. Most of the social development that began in the fourth week, such as

pack movement and playful fighting, becomes much more pronounced in the eighth. Combative play becomes more intense as a means of developing the ranking order of dominance and subordinateness. This scuffle for rank has a lasting effect, resulting in timid dogs, even-tempered dogs, or overly aggressive dogs.

For these reasons, a number of researchers have concluded that a dog experiencing human handling as a socializing technique should be removed from the litter and taken to its new home with a human family no later than the beginning of the eighth week. This time frame, however, is a matter of opinion. Some breeders disagree and feel the puppies should remain with the litter until the end of the twelfth week. By removing the puppies in the eighth week the last vestiges of weaning are automatically ended but the effects of a developing dominance order are avoided. Assuming the puppy has been handled since the fourth week, it is now ready to make the transition to living as a pet and accepting some small amount of obedience training, as well as the beginning of housebreaking.

At this stage of the dog's life he has the capacity to become an engaging, well-trained companion, providing he is allowed to develop self-confidence as an individual dog with worth and value. Do not allow the young dog to be alone or isolated for long periods of time. Give the pup a great deal of positive attention. Conduct short obedience training sessions that allow for the opportunity for much-needed praise. At the end of the twelfth week, your dog enters his juvenile period ready for complete obedience training and all the pleasures of being an adult dog.

—4—

THE DOG
AND YOUR FAMILY

I once asked a psychologist, "Who needs children, anyway? What is the point to it all? Do human beings really feel incomplete if they fail to become parents?" The older man smiled warmly and replied, "No, not necessarily. But a child gives us one more person to love and feel better for doing so." Now that I have three children I no longer ask such foolish questions, because the good doctor's answer is more valid than ever. And you know what? The same is true about dogs.

Once a dog is taken into your home it is an integral part of the family whether you planned for that or not. Looking for the essence of family life is like peeling away the layers of an onion. It is not until we get to the tiny piece in the center that we recognize that the peeled layers are the true essence of the onion. Whatever exists within and around your family are the parts that make up the whole of it. For better or for worse, the dog you have taken in, like the child you have borne, the spouse you have committed to, or the parent you live with, is a part of your life. It adds or subtracts, strengthens or weakens your day-to-day existence. It cannot be ignored. Even if the dog was for the kids, its impact on every member of the family is quite great. The friendship, love, and responsibility of a dog are a shared experience.

WHOSE DOG IS IT?

It really doesn't matter for whom the dog was purchased. Dogs are independent creatures in that they will focus their attention on one or more persons as they desire, and there is no controlling that. There is a misconception that the dog will belong exclusively to the one who feeds him or pays the most attention. Certainly, the person who offers essential goods and services has an edge, but not to the exclusion of everyone else in the family. Sometimes the person who pays the least attention to the dog nonetheless becomes the focus of the dog's affection. No one knows for sure why this happens. Some dogs are attracted to the strong, silent type. It could simply be that the dog likes one person's odor more than another's.

The point is that a new dog's presence sets in motion a rippling effect within the family structure. The focus will certainly change, at least for a while, and the spotlight will focus on everything the dog does. If there is more than one child, the youngest may not garner all the concern and fuss that he or she is accustomed to receiving. The dog takes some of that attention away, at least temporarily. Some relationships will be altered, creating new alliances and dissolving old ones. Emotions can run high. It's as if a new baby were brought home from the hospital, causing joy, concern, and thinly veiled anxiety.

Getting a dog for one child when there are others in the

family is not recommended. This situation sets up a potential for dissension that can lead to deeply felt resentments. Anyone who has ever lived with more than one child knows that peace in the family rests on very shaky treaties be-

tween siblings. Arguing over the use of the telephone or a favored toy is bad enough in its own shallow futility. But the overlap of emotions connected with a love object creates intense feelings that can shake boulders. No, I suggest that you acquire a *family* dog rather than a personal possession for one child over another. For this reason alone, dogs make poor birthday gifts. If you want to give a puppy as a gift, then do it during a holiday when the dog can be a gift for all.

Often a new dog will attract a member of the family who has an intense need for exclusive attention, love, and companionship. But the dog must be treated as a member of the family, belonging to himself. Still, activities involving care of the dog can be considered exclusive time spent with him. It will help get feeding, grooming, training, and walking chores accomplished and satisfy the family member's desire for exclusive attention. You'll get two needs satisfied for the price of one. Even if you have one child, it is still a good policy to refer to the new dog as a member of the family rather than as a personal possession of the child. If your child has a psychological need of things that are exclusively his or hers for the sake of identity (and most do), let it be an object, a room, or a monogrammed item of clothing. But allow the dog to be the family dog. It's a matter of mental hygiene for both humans *and* canines.

NAMING THE DOG

The first activity connected with a new dog concerns selecting a name for him. This should be a very pleasant task, although for some it leads to the first of many conflicts. I would make this a family decision rather than the choice of one child. The person who selects the name can very easily take possession of the dog in his or her mind and get off to a bad start. Although choosing a name for a dog seems to be such a simple, innocent task, it really is important. The objective is to avoid a major conflict. Choosing a name right away promotes self-confidence in the dog and facilitates training. Everyone has to refer to the animal by the same name lest the dog suffer from an identity crisis.

Convene a family council and agree to come to a shared decision. You can make a game of the process by having everyone in the family participate in the selection. Have each person think of a name category, such as TV cartoon characters, historical figures, Greek mythology, geography, or names of friends, relatives, or celebrities. Once a category is chosen, subdivide it into other categories such as dates, time, nostalgia, or contemporary. You may wish to have everyone choose one or more letters to create a name or spell someone's name backwards. The point is to allow each person to participate in the process. Then it can be truthfully stated that everyone named the dog. It sets the right tone.

Suggestions for Naming Your Dog

The dog's characteristics lead to good names.

Big Boy	Curly	Patches	Spats
Big Girl	Flash	Peaches	Spike
Birdie	Flicker	Pearl	Splash
Blackie	Floppy	Pickles	Spot
Blinky	Gloves	Red	Spud
Bubbles	Goldy	Salty	Tangerine
Chief	Jazzy	Silver	Toes
Chips	Jigger	Slats	Wag
Chum	Lemon Drop	Slick	Wheezy
Cinnamon	Lightning	Smoothie	Whiskers
Cocoa	Lovelady	Sorrowful	Wings
Coffee	Macaroon	Sparks	

Favored cities make unique names.

Albany	Cheyenne	Manhattan	Salem
Albuquerque	Cleveland	Memphis	Sandusky
Altoona	Dallas	Miami	San Jose
Atlanta	Daytona	Missoula	San Juan
Baltimore	Denver	Nashua	Toledo
Bismarck	El Paso	Nome	Toronto
Boise	Fayette	Paducah	Tucson
Boston	Honolulu	Pittsburgh	Tulsa
Brooklyn	Houston	Portland	Washington
Buffalo	Independence	Providence	Wayne
Calgary	Levittown	Reno	Wichita

And who says you can't have two or even three names?

Bart Simpson	Jean-Luc Picard	Miss Piggy
Big Bird	Johnny Carson	Mr. T
Clark Kent	Kermit the Dog	Olivia Newton-John
David Letterman	Lady Macbeth	Ralph Waldo Emerson
Gary Coleman	Lois Lane	Ronald McDonald
He-Man	Michael Jackson	Twyla Tharp
Jay Leno	Mickey Mouse	Wonder Dog

There is educational value in naming a dog from the classics.

SHAKESPEARE

Antony	Coriolanus	Julius	Polonius
Ariel	Cressida	Kate	Portia
Banquo	Cymbeline	King Lear	Prospero
Beatrice	Dogberry	Laertes	Puck
Benvolio	Falstaff	Macbeth	Richard II
Brutus	Gertrude	Macduff	Roderigo
Caesar	Gloucester	Mercutio	Romeo
Calpurnia	Hamlet	Montague	Sir Toby
Capulet	Henry IV	Ophelia	Timon
Cassius	Horatio	Othello	Titania
Cato	Hotspur	Pericles	Titus
Cleopatra	Iago	Petruchio	Troilus
Cordelia	Juliet	Pistol	Yorick

GREEK MYTHOLOGY

Achilles	Eros	Midas	Poseidon
Agamemnon	Eurydice	Narcissus	Prometheus
Andromeda	Hades	Nemesis	Proteus
Aphrodite	Helen	Odysseus	Psyche
Apollo	Helios	Olympus	Pygmalion
Artemis	Heracles	Orion	Telemachus
Athena	Hermes	Orpheus	Theseus
Atlas	Hippolytus	Pan	Titan
Centaur	Icarus	Pandora	Troy
Demeter	Jason	Perseus	Typhon
Dionysus	Medea	Phaedra	Uranus
Echo	Medusa	Pluto	Zeus

POETRY

Barefoot	Glory	Mandalay	Shadow
Bells	Gulliver	Milton	Skylark
Boy Blue	Guppy	Naughty Boy	Sonnet
Captain	Jabberwock	Nightingale	Sweeney
Charms	Joy	Peekaboo	Sweet Afton
Cummerbund	Just So	Prufrock	Taro
Deever	Kangaroo	Quangle	Tiger
Fog	Kubla Khan	Raven	Trees
Frankie (and	Lamb	Rubaiyat	Walrus
Johnny)	Lochinvar	Seven	Xanadu

Entire books exist about naming pets and show dogs. I hope these suggestions will help in the family decision about what to name the dog. The lists are meant merely to stimulate the imagination and to give you an inkling of the possibilities. One could look for a dog name in the days of the week, months of the year, types of food (radish, berry, pizza, ham bone, soufflé, hot dog, spaghetti), from crossword puzzles, or from any other source that the human imagination can land on. Allow everyone to get involved in the process, and that certainly includes everyone in the family, but especially the kids.

THE DOG AS BEST FRIEND

Although it is very rewarding for a child to feel competent enough to assume the responsibilities of dog care, these responsibilities must not be thrust on anyone. If you get a dog for the family it should be fun. Making a chore out of it right away is a mistake, as is making it a success or failure situation. Allow the family to enjoy the animal without assigning responsibilities. This freedom permits the development of relationships between everyone and the dog. The pet should be introduced to the family and then be allowed to play with each family member (in a way that isn't overly tiring).

Far too many parents set up rules and regulations governing the dog's care and the children's responsibilities before the animal even enters the picture. These preconditions may or may not work out because of the dog and because of the kids. It takes a potentially lighthearted, mirthful occasion and casts a needless, serious shadow over the event. Giving the kids a dog can be a meaningful experience and still be fun at the same time. Allowing your kids to have a good time with their new dog is more important than any "educational" or "growth development" factors. That all comes later. As a matter of fact, most kids begin to set their own rules and limitations on matters pertaining to the dog. Allow for the possibility of the children themselves sorting out which responsibilities they want. That's a much more meaningful development for both dog and children.

The relationship with the dog will grow and deepen quickly as the child decides what she wants to do for the family pet. Most children that I have seen in this situation want very much to be involved in everything that affects the dog. The wise parent will sit back and let it happen. As a child volunteers for a chore (hooray!), praise, encourage, and help her in order to promote a feeling of accomplishment. This sense of accomplishment will create the proper motivation for the child to continue to perform useful tasks. Do not be disappointed if the child becomes bored or loses interest in any one aspect of the dog's care. When that happens it is time to suggest a different chore. The success of having dogs and kids live together lies in the development of their relationship. It is desirable for a child to be a dog's best friend and, to a lesser degree, the other way around. A growing, prosperous relationship between child and dog can only occur if the initial contact is pleasurable.

THE DOG AS RIVAL

A dog, like the arrival of a new child, can inadvertently become the symbol of established friction. Most brothers and sisters compete with one another for parental attention and favor. The competition can be comical, serious, or totally absurd in its forms and directions. Bickering siblings tend to demand absolute equality and parity from their harassed and hassled parents. The combination of one dog and several kids has the makings of a potential nightmare for a mother and father who have had it up to here.

It would be wise always to walk the dog out of the competitive storm at the first sign of clouds on the horizon. Only a psychotherapist could use the outcome of such conflicts as a clue to the underlying meaning of this behavior. At this point it is best for the dog not to be the focus of your children's anger. It's not really good for either the children or the dog. Without getting involved in their argument, you can inform them that they are upsetting the dog (not to mention their bedraggled parents). Although problems between siblings vary, this one has something to do with their ability to share. The children must be told that the dog is to be shared by the entire family and that they mustn't tear the animal apart. Schedules, appointments, and the ability to take turns with the dog are essential. You might even convince combative siblings to play with the animal together.

Sometimes, unwitting parents find themselves the rival of the dog for the children's attention. Even more seriously, children sometimes compete with the dog for a parent's attention. These are situations that are easy to adjust but must be taken care of before serious emotional problems develop. It is almost inevitable that jealousy develops where family dynamics are concerned. But remember, dogs will accept whatever attention you decide you can give them. They start out neutral and can be brought back to neutral from any imbalance that grows. If the dog figures into any feelings of jealousy between the kids, it is time to sort it all out by having a family talk and clearing the air. Just keep pointing out that the dog belongs to himself and is to be enjoyed by everyone in the family.

THE DOG AS PROTECTOR

There was once a situation in which a Labrador Retriever kept diving into the family swimming pool to rescue the young swimmers whether they needed it or not. Some dogs are much more territorial than others and regard the people in their lives as part of their work. On the whole, it is a good kind of problem. Dogs that will protect home and family are worth their weight in gold. They are the kind of dog we all dream about . . . well, almost all. Even small terriers and, believe it or not, some of the toy breeds offer a great deal of protection. Terriers and some toy breeds are highly sensitive to the comings and goings of strangers in their territory and will alert the family at the slightest hint of irregularity. Often this behavior is a nuisance because of the barking and yapping it causes at any hour of the day or night. Don't expect a ten-pound dog to knock a burglar over while you call the police. But I have heard of situations where these mighty mites have opened arteries in the ankle, thus driving off would-be assailants. That's the good news.

The bad news is when a dog attacks strangers who are in your home on business or for some other legitimate purpose. And then there are the visits from relatives, friends, and neighbors. There is nothing worse than a twelve-year-old kid getting attacked by your dog when coming to your house to see a friend. An overly protective or highly territorial dog will cut down on everyone's social life and could even provoke the postal service to discontinue delivering your mail.

If you have a dog of this type you must become aware of certain awful possibilities. Dogs can make protection decisions that are irrational and deadly. This sad fact is especially true of breeds of the Working Group, which include Collies, Bouviers, Boxers, German Shepherd Dogs, and Great Danes. Potential problems may also arise with some hounds and sporting dogs, such as Weimaraners and Chesapeake Bay Retrievers. Occasionally, an overly protective dog comes from a breed not noted for this behavior. All aggressive dogs (regardless of breed) can be dangerous. You must pay careful attention to a dog and learn to recognize this trait for what it is.

There are several courses for the owners of such dogs to take. First and foremost, have the dog obedience trained by a professional. I would *not* recommend a training class (more than one dog being trained at a time) for a very aggressive dog or a course given at home by a member of the family. This job is for a skilled obedience trainer who can provide hands-on, one-to-one training. Training classes are appropriate for dogs with no behavior problems. At the end of the training the dog must obey all members of the family instantly. The next step is to become diligent about

using the dog's leash outdoors and whenever a stranger comes to the house (unless the dog is confined to another room). Never allow this kind of dog free to roam when it is out of the house. And finally, do not allow anyone, especially children, to engage in play that encourages, teaches, or provokes aggressive behavior. Avoid tug-of-war, biting games, chewing and mouthing games, excessive chasing, and cornering. Use your common sense.

THE CHILD AS PROTECTOR

A seldom-considered aspect of pet ownership concerns the protection of the animal. It is all too obvious that small puppies and even young dogs need protection. They are just babies and totally dependent on us for everything from

warmth to food to shelter. But adult dogs need various forms of protection, too, and they can be helped in part by children. Many dogs can be saved from their own self-destructive behavior. For example, dogs that chew on their paws cause themselves skin problems and infections. A child can make the dog stop such behavior with a simple command (assuming the dog is obedience trained). Getting into things for the purpose of snacking is detrimental to the dog. Rooting through the garbage is not only disgusting, it is also bad for digestive stability. Swallowing a splintery bone has the potential for inflicting internal puncture wounds. Some human foods are not tolerated by a dog's sensitive stomach; indeed, they are barely tolerated by the human stomach. Because children pay more attention to dogs, they are far more capable of observing their behavior and stopping them from hurting themselves.

The worst thing a dog can do to himself is get embroiled in a fight with another dog. Although males are more likely to fight other males, do not discount the female penchant for this destructive activity. Dogs can become severely wounded or even lose their lives in such skirmishes. Moreover, a human trying to stop a dogfight can also be wounded seriously in the process. Fights can and should be avoided and children can help.

When children handle dogs they must be made aware of the possibility for fighting when one dog meets another. Inform your child about dogfighting and the need to try to avoid it. Tell him or her that strange dogs meeting for the first time are quite likely to challenge each other to determine who is "top dog" and whose territory they are in. The dogs must not be allowed to get close to each other if there seems to be the slightest hint of aggressive behavior. Signs of aggression include hard staring, pricked ears, cautious and deliberate body language, low-throated growls, and bared teeth through snarling lips. Two dogs meeting on the street, at the end of their leashes, may start out sweetly. In an instant, however, things can change and they may go for each other's throats. Children can protect their dogs from these incidents by watching for the first sign of aggressive behavior. Instruct your child to pull the dog away and to keep on walking. If two dogs begin to fight, children should only pull the dogs apart with the leash. No one should step between the dogs or place their hands anywhere on either dog's body. Holler at them, give corrections and commands, even douse them with water. However, parents must advise their children to prevent getting bitten by avoiding any physical contact with fighting dogs. Also, note that it is a good idea for a child to leave his dog at home when playing at a friend's house, especially if the friend also has a dog. Separating two fighting dogs is neither an easy nor a safe task for either a child or an adult.

Prevention can save the dog from himself, and even a child can do it. Part of a child's love of animals is wrapped up in a desire to protect them. That protective compassion should be encouraged to blossom.

YOUR CHILD'S ATTITUDE ABOUT DOGS

What is it about animals that is so attractive to children? Some grown-ups believe that young children consider animals to be disguised human beings, thus making it "safe" for children to express their true feelings:

"The bear [Daddy?] is ferocious and will eat me up unless I get away."
"The bunny [Mommy?] is soft and feels nice. It will love me and be my friend."
"Puppies [a young brother or sister?] are the dickens and should be punished."
"Kitty cats [himself?] are naughty but too smart to get caught."
"My dog [big brother?] likes me and will bite you if you try to be mean to me."

Occasionally a child will trade places with a pet and then be free to say what's really on her mind:

"I am going to jump all over you and lick your face
and then you'll have to look at me."
"I'll bite your fingers off and that'll teach you not to
spank me."

Sometimes a pet dog is regarded as a strong protector
controlled by the child, ready to do its master's bidding.
This belief may allow the child to feel more secure with
those who are frightening or more dominant such as an
older brother or sister.

Obviously, there is a great deal of fantasy connected to
a child's attitude toward a pet dog. Dogs make incredibly
dynamic *huggies* or love objects. A sweet-natured dog that
will curl up with a child is infinitely more effective and
attractive than a stuffed toy or an old baby blanket. A dog
can make a terrific substitute parent, one that can be cut
down to size or easily controlled when desired. Some dogs
are even thought of as super heroes who can save the child
from danger or feelings of loneliness and despair. Children
often endow their pet dog with magical powers that enable
it to fly away at night and live out incredible adventures,
returning home in the morning as a conquering hero. Try to
tell a small child that his dog doesn't have the same feelings
that he does and you'll be regarded as a lunatic. As a matter
of fact, most children believe that their dog knows exactly
what they are thinking.

When my oldest boy was four he believed his dog could
speak to other dogs in what he called *Doglish*. For a year he
tried to learn that language. I believe he succeeded. When
children feel bad they often believe their dogs feel the same
way. The reverse is also true. What it all seems to mean is
that children identify with small animals much more easily
than with complex humans who "have their own problems."
Sometimes a very young pet owner sits her dog down,
pours him an imaginary cup of tea, and holds a thirty-

minute conversation with the charitable guest. Only a dog
will sit still for that. A smart parent will try to eavesdrop on
such a conversation. He may learn how his child feels about
the quality of his parenting.

It is generally much easier for a child to express and
receive affection from an animal. Young boys tend to regard
hugging and kissing from their moms as "mush." However,
a dog can plant a kiss and it's called "licking the face."
Dogs are so direct in their pursuit of contact with humans
that they easily cut through the typical barriers set up by
children.

DIFFERENCES BETWEEN
DOG AND CHILD BEHAVIOR

The only similarity between dog behavior and child behavior is the powerful impact of early experience on adult
behavior. That which young dogs are exposed to will definitely affect elements of adult behavior such as adaptability
to humans and animals, learning abilities, emotional stability, and self-confidence. The same could be said about
young children.

With the exception of guide dogs for the blind and other
serious workers, dogs at twelve to eighteen months of age
are pretty much what they will be for the rest of their lives.
This, of course, is not the case for children. They are in a
constant, ongoing state of intellectual, emotional, psychological, and physical growth for many years. Every week
seems to bring a new development in the life of a child, and
that is important to understand, particularly as it relates to
living with a dog. Parents must expect constant change with
regard to a child's relationship with a dog. A child may
begin a week loving the dog with enthusiasm and wanting
to do every single thing connected with the dog's care. By
the end of the week he may be totally disinterested. It's

difficult to know why this happens. I do not believe in explanations as simple as a "limited attention span" or "boredom." I suspect that the child has experienced some transitional phase of growth and has refocused on another aspect of his or her life to the exclusion of the dog. This does not mean that the love affair with the animal is finished. It means that the dog has been temporarily placed on hold, and parents should be tolerant. Do not get rid of the dog. Take over the dog's care until the child is ready to relate to it again. Or, insist that the child continue with certain chores such as walking and feeding. Tailor the approach you take to the emotional state of the child and to your "style" of parenting.

It is worth mentioning that dog behavior is very different from human behavior. Dogs cannot function without a "pack leader," and function best when that leader maintains a dominant manner. Children, on the other hand, must be encouraged to strive for their maximum potential, and that requires self-confidence, independence, a healthy self-image, and the ability to risk failure. It is paradoxical that dogs reach their potential as human pets in an environment that would be detrimental to children. Dogs accept the world as they find it and seek their place in it. Children look for new worlds in order to create their place. Each, in his way, is correct. It is the wise parent who relates to dogs and children in the manner needed for each. Children and dogs are, indeed, separate creatures.

THE HUMANE CHILD

If your child respects his dog as a living creature with a right to live a life free of pain and oppressive behavior, he or she is what the world needs the most. Do not underestimate the power for good that lies in the hearts of humane children. Loving animals and respecting their needs for a decent life are acts that children can take with them into adulthood, and isn't that a fine thing for both our children and the rest of us?

It is not far-fetched to believe that humane and kindly behavior toward animals can become a way of behaving toward all. But the value of decency must be taught and promoted by a child's parents in word and deed and example. What you *say* and what you *do* have an enormous influence on your child. If you hit a dog, your child will hit a dog. If you are abusive, then your child will learn to be abusive. Although children love animals because they identify with their innocence, they also experience moments of anger, rage, and a desire to strike out. It is a parent's responsibility to see to it that these irrational bursts of minor violence are never directed at the family dog, just as

they are not to be tolerated against any other member of the family.

Those of us who are in the trenches, trying to raise children to be upstanding, decent human beings, never forget that the kids are watching and learning from what they see and hear. It isn't easy. Being nice to your dog as an example for your children is not hard and goes a long, long way to make the world a better place.

THE FAMILY DOG AS TEACHER

By bringing a dog into your home, you are introducing children to a living thing with needs corresponding to those of humans; i.e., food, water, shelter, and love and affection. But your pet dog also serves as a valuable teaching tool, capturing and holding a child's attention far longer than books or diagrams. There are endless possibilities for parents, as the partners of teachers, to apply dog-related lessons toward the personal and academic development of their children. With the help of a fine reference entitled "Professor Pet," written and produced by the American Pet Products Manufacturers Association and distributed by the Pet Information Bureau, I give you many examples of ways to use your dog as a stimulus to learning.

Defining right and wrong. Children remember best that which they have learned through experience or direct observation. Although a dog's actions are not necessarily indicative of proper human behavior, certain situations can draw attention to lessons to be learned from them. When a larger dog dominates a smaller dog, a natural instinct, the child may be taught how unacceptable this is among humans. Help your child to understand that animals are motivated by instincts, whereas humans act according to instincts *and* complex reasoning.

Getting along with others. Through observation, kids can be taught how animals interact with each other—those of the same species and those totally unrelated to each other. Initiate a discussion of how animals behave with each other with an emphasis on why they do what they do. Then compare that behavior with the children's own personal relationships so that they understand the similarities and differences between the interactive behavior of people and animals.

Sex education. When a child asks, "Where did I come from and how did I get here?"—questions that are inevitable—you may find the answers are made easier through an analogy with your pet.

Life and death. Just as birth is a mysterious subject to small children, death is a concept even fewer children can begin to comprehend. The natural death of a neighbor's dog can become an ideal opportunity for a parent to begin a discussion about the subject. Use this opportunity to explain what caused the animal to die, the physical realities of dying, the naturalness of death, and so on.

Survival. Even domesticated animals preserve their keen instinct to survive. They rely on a system of defense mechanisms that is activated when their security is threatened. Have a discussion in which the natural defenses of dogs are compared with the deliberate actions taken by humans to preserve their well-being.

Independence. Animals demonstrate their independence from their mothers much earlier than humans do, and although a dog remains dependent on its owner for basic essentials, it still displays a sense of independence. Lead a discussion of the ways in which a dog takes care of itself and how children can display their independence at home and at school.

Companionship, affection, love. As children care for and play with a dog, they will develop emotional attachments to the animal that can be related to their feelings for other people. Discussions could center on what love means to each child, how his or her feelings for the pet differ from and/or resemble feelings toward parents and friends, how the child imagines the dog feels about him or her, and so on.

Working with basic shapes. Have your child observe the dog and pick out basic shapes from various parts of the body and coat pattern such as circles, rectangles, and squares.

Decorating the dog's space. Have your child complete a project in which she draws pictures and/or constructs a mobile with dogs on it. The pictures could depict aspects of the dog's life such as his bowl, leash, and pillow. Use the artwork as a way of decorating the walls around the dog's corner of the room.

Mural painting. Cover a wall with paper and have all the kids draw themselves playing with their dog. Also, encourage them to illustrate elements of responsible pet ownership such as feeding and providing affection.

Drawing from live models. There is no better model for drawing than the family dog. Wait until the dog is taking a nap and then set your child to work with paper and crayons or paint.

Animal environments. After discussing what a dog's environment is like in the wild (you may draw from information available about the wolf), have the kids draw their dog in the woods, the mountains, along the timberline, or in the jungle.

Dog collage. Collect old magazines, box tops, string, leaves, and so on in order to provide materials that relate in some way to the children's dog and its life. Encourage the kids to create collages in which they paste the materials to a piece of cardboard. Have the kids include a drawing or photograph of the dog.

Making gifts for the dog. For Christmas tell the children to make a stocking for the dog or for the dogs of friends and neighbors. Have the children make toys with which to fill the stockings.

Writing stories. Suggest to your children that they write a story about the family dog and the adventures it has had or may have had. "A Day in the Life of" your dog is a perfect story to write. An interesting and possibly revealing story for your child to write would concern itself with what it would be like to trade places with the dog and live its life for a while.

Dog poems. Ask your kids to write some poems about their dog. Having the poems read aloud can be fun, especially if there is an audience. You might want to read aloud some famous dog poems to the children. Look through the works of poets such as Ogden Nash, A. A. Milne, Don Marquis, and Stephen Foster. Talk to your librarian to learn about other poets who have written dog poems.

Read a dog story. Help your child select a book about a dog and tell her to read it in preparation for a quiz game. If your child does not read, then read the book to her. When the child has completed the book, have her summarize the story and identify the most important information she obtained from it. Ask questions about the book, as in a quiz show, and award prizes. You can use the book for a spelling bee or even to help identify verbs, nouns, and other parts of speech. The dog story will make such excrcises more interesting.

Animal role-playing. Ask your kids and their friends to put together a play in which the roles are those of animals, including the family dog. Have the kids portray the animals' feelings and thoughts and have them imitate the animals' actions and interactions. This activity should be great fun.

Pet photography. Have your kids photograph the dog with a simple camera. First, you may wish to take a photo of the kids and the dog together. Next, have the children operate the camera, snapping photos of the dog as it engages in daily activities. Start a photo album containing pictures of the dog. As an alternative, hang photos on a wall and hold an exhibit for friends, relatives, and neighbors. An opening of a dog photo exhibit makes for a wonderful social event.

Foreign language and culture. If you read about the history of your purebred dog, you will find that in all likelihood the breed originated in another country. You may use this fact as a springboard to learning about the language and culture of foreign countries. You may then wish to discuss which dogs came from which countries, thus taking the opportunity to introduce your children to the language and culture of various societies.

Animal origins. Lead your children to understand that dogs come from areas all around the globe. Have the kids research where the family dog (and their friends' dogs) originated, what year the dogs were first mentioned in history books or logged in science books, what other animals the dog is related to, what its ancestors were like, and so on. You may wish to encourage the children to gather their facts as part of a quiz in which a prize will be awarded to the child who answers the most questions correctly.

Pets' service to mankind. Tell your children that many animals were first kept as pets because they provided a service of some kind to humans. Have your children learn what type of service your dog (and other animals, too) may have provided.

Working dogs. Explain to your children that many dogs are "employed" by their owners to perform a specific job. Explore with your kids the types of jobs that dogs perform (i.e., guarding, herding, aiding the visually impaired) and how these dogs are trained for their specific tasks.

Pets and climate. Have your children learn about the different weather and temperature preferences of various dog breeds and discuss what characteristics enable the dogs to live in the climates they do. You may wish to broaden this discussion with an investigation of how humans and other animals adapt to a variety of climatic conditions.

Pets in history. Famous people often had famous pets, from the royal dogs of Chinese emperors to the many dogs of George Washington and Teddy Roosevelt. See how many noted dogs (and other pets) your child can uncover throughout history.

Learning about measurement. To teach children about measurement, show them how to measure the amounts used in feeding the family dog, the size and weight of the dog, the size of the dog's living quarters, and so on.

The metric system. All the measurements used in maintaining the dog can be converted to metric amounts. Help the kids create a chart of conversion formulas and equivalent measurements. Many metric weights and measurements can be found printed on bags and boxes of dog food.

Introduction to accounting. Lessons in accounting can be illustrated by the amount of time and money needed to care for the family dog. Explain the basics of debits and credits, and keep an accounting ledger for the costs involving the dog. (Note: examples of debits may include the cost of food and visits to the veterinarian; examples of credits may include profits from operating a dog walking service.)

Working with graphs. Older kids can learn how to work with graphs by monitoring the dog's weight, food intake, maintenance costs, growth, and so on.

Health care. By introducing children to the proper nutritional requirements of their dog, they will develop a better understanding of their own nutritional requirements. Have them make a poster of basic foods that their dog needs to remain healthy. Then have them design a poster with the basic food groups humans need to remain healthy.

Grooming care. Some pets, such as cats, groom themselves, while others need to have their owners do it for them. The latter group includes the family dog. Discuss what is required to keep the dog groomed and clean. Note the benefits of keeping a dog well groomed and clean, and relate these benefits to the children's personal hygiene.

Your dog's senses. All dogs have the same senses as humans. However, some kinds of dogs possess one or more senses that are more developed than other dogs. For example, Bloodhounds, Beagles, and Dachshunds have a greater sense of smell than other breeds. Greyhounds, Whippets, and Salukis have especially keen senses of sight. These heightened sensory abilities developed in order to help the animals adapt to the particular challenges imposed by their environments. Lead your children in a discussion about the strength of senses among various dogs as well as humans. This discussion can be enhanced by showing your children various objects and having them close their eyes to identify the objects using their senses of smell, touch, and taste.

Protection. Start a discussion about how dogs protect themselves in the wilderness. Note how dogs prepare for seasonal changes by shedding in the summer and growing a new coat in the winter. Talk about how the dog would defend itself from predators if it were in its natural environment.

Anatomy. Have your children conduct research in order to learn about dog anatomy. Encourage them to make a diagram of the dog's anatomy in which the parts are labeled. Then have the children compare the dog's body structure to that of humans and other animals and ask them to point out distinctive characteristics such as the dog's tail, the length of its body, and its snout.

Communication. Communication is a vital part of any creature's existence and dogs have the ability to communicate with or without sound. Discuss with your children how your dog communicates with other dogs and with humans. Compare the dog's methods of communication to the types of communication used by humans. Lead your children to understand how human language skills afford us a special place in the animal kingdom.

These activities represent some of the very many ways you can use the dog itself as an aid to your children's education. More than that, these activities are fun and will serve you and the children quite well on rainy days when kids "have nothing to do." Learning and having fun are all part of having a dog in the family.

—5—

HOUSEBREAKING AND OTHER DELIGHTS

Children and dogs have much in common when it comes to toilet training and housebreaking. When both species are very young they cannot control themselves to any degree because of a lack of development of the muscles that open and close the floodgates. Sphincter control does not begin to develop in a child until roughly the third year of life. Thank God, those muscles in a dog develop far earlier. A three-month-old puppy can go for eight hours through the night, under the right circumstances, without eliminating. If the puppy is confined in a dog crate, denied food or water at bedtime, and not disturbed, he will not soil because his body won't have the need. Neither infants nor puppies have a concept of using a specific place that is more desirable than another to relieve themselves. Housebreaking and toilet training are both learned processes based on environmental control, eating schedules, instruction, repetition, and, to some degree, imitative behavior. Most child experts tell us not to rush the toilet training process at all and to begin somewhere around two-and-a-half or three years of age. Pediatricians are famous for saying, "No child ever wet his pants at his college commencement." However, puppies must be housebroken at a much earlier age. In terms of physical development, a three-month-old puppy is possibly equivalent to a three- or four-year-old human. No one bothers putting diapers on a dog, so housebreaking is an aesthetic necessity. To wait longer is to make the task more difficult.

In our society one's sensibilities seem to be assaulted by the sight of or even the mention of our bodily wastes. We choke with inhibition, embarrassment, anger, or inarticulateness over this subject. Some giggle while others regress to "Boop-boop-a-doop." The subject of bodily wastes provokes a wide variety of emotional responses in people, both expressed and suppressed. And yet mothers (and some enlightened fathers) have been dealing with the subject in their dear children for many years with resignation and dignified good humor. It would be irrational to raise one or more children from infancy on and yet feel upset about dealing with a dog's eliminative realities.

Once parents understand they are going to have to change soiled diapers for a minimum of two or three years per child, they settle down and accept the situation. It would be unthinkable and quite destructive to express great anger or to hit a child for "having an accident" during toilet training. Well, the same is true for puppies. If you want a healthy, housebroken dog that is a pleasant creature, not cowed or frightened of you, then proper housebreaking technique, coupled with a basic knowledge of canine eliminative behavior, is important to you.

There are some very distinct differences between children and dogs as to what elimination means to each. Obviously, toilet training for the child and housebreaking for the dog require quite different approaches and techniques.

Children toilet train, if handled properly, because they want to be like mommy, daddy, brother, and sister. Dogs appreciate housebreaking because they are genetically programmed to eliminate as far away as possible from where they eat and sleep. Nature has provided this behavior for the dog as a means of avoiding detection in the wild by predators. The nest in which newborn puppies snuggle is kept clean because the mother ingests what little waste matter there is. As the weeks go by, young puppies instinctively crawl out of the nest to relieve themselves, and ultimately return to the same spots they have already soiled.

When a child finally begins using the toilet and gives up diapers for training pants, it is a source of pride and accomplishment. It is one of those milestones in a child's life that signifies that one is becoming a "big boy" or "big girl." From then on, going to the toilet is simply an aspect of human digestion. Not so for a dog. As dogs leave puppyhood they begin marking, or scent posting. It is a way of claiming one's territory, proclaiming dominance (without the actual presence of another dog), and a means of communication between males and females. So, one can see that urine and feces are extremely important to dogs and serve far greater uses than the mere elimination of waste matter.

There are two facts of canine elimination that are of vital importance to the family that wishes to housebreak a dog. First, confining the dog to a small area when not closely supervised utilizes his instinct to avoid soiling his nest. Second, allow the dog to discover scent post areas outside the house; you will be using the dog's attraction to the posted odors of canine body waste to great advantage. The dog will return to the same spots to eliminate time and time again because of the scent, even if it is his own. Dogs in the neighborhood will mark the same spots and then your dog will mark over theirs in a sort of battle-by-proxy.

It's all quite harmless and very useful for housebreaking purposes.

When housebreaking your dog, you may wish to consider allowing the children to become involved in the process. Whether or not that is a good idea depends on the age of the child, his or her attitude toward urination and defecation, and how much responsibility he or she can handle. Certainly, all children can learn something by simply watching the housebreaking process as it's carried out by the adults. I would say a child of ten years or older can actually help out. Housebreaking a dog consists of confinement, a rigid feeding schedule, supervising the dog when he is not confined, walking the dog or taking him to his newspapers, correcting him, and praising him. The aspects of housebreaking that your child can handle can be determined only by you. It would be a bad choice to allow a ten-year-old to walk a large, untrained dog in city streets. It would be a good idea to decide ahead of time which aspect of housebreaking your kids can handle and then to stick with that, assuming it works out.

If your dog is past two months of age, he is biologically ready for housebreaking. Although training is not a voluntary activity, the dog will do much better if your emphasis is on praise for what he does properly rather than harshness for his mistakes. Do not misunderstand: a dog must be *corrected* when he does the wrong thing, but let us not make it a losing battle for him. As with a child, the more the dog loses, the less confidence he has in himself. To be sure, much of dog training consists of behavior modification and conditioning its responses. But we must not ignore the dog as an individual entity with its own personality and perception of the world. To rub his nose in his own mess is to tear a page from the Joseph Stalin school of behavior. Even a dog that poops on the floor deserves to be treated with kindness and understanding. If your dog is a *sooner*

(sooner mess the floor than go outside), don't take it personally. It has nothing to do with spite or the dog's teaching you a lesson for leaving him alone. Forget all that ill-informed nonsense.

There are only a few reasons why a dog messes on the floor. The first and foremost reason is simply that the dog has not been housebroken properly or completely. The second reason is medical. A sick dog often has no control over himself. This is true of dogs with worms, upset stomachs, viruses, infections, or bladder problems. Many old dogs lose control as well. Some breeds or groups of breeds are genetically prone to incontinence and are difficult to housebreak. This is not to say that they cannot be housebroken. But it means that these breeds are more difficult to housebreak and require a rigid training program that is administered vigorously. Some of these breeds were developed to live outdoors on their own or outdoors in a kennel with a large pack. Such an animal is too busy minding the store to be concerned with carefully avoiding house soiling. He must be conditioned for such behavior, and that requires more effort from the trainer than normal.

When a dog messes on your bed, the floor, or under the carpet, it does not, in my opinion, have anything to do with spite. Revenge is an art confined to the madness of obsessed human beings. Dogs are much nicer than that. No, I hate to spoil all that funny cocktail party chitchat, but dogs soil the house when you are gone because they are ridden with anxiety. They are not expressing some form of primitive rage laced with the desire to get even. Your absence may give your dog a form of identity crisis in that he has no idea if you're ever coming back to feed him, to nurture him, to make him feel secure. It is quite possible that his urine and feces are a message-sending technique or simply a physical expression of fear. Some dogs, especially toy breeds, pee on your bed when you're gone. Your bed is the place with the strongest human odor. Although it is irrational, there is a sort of dog logic to leaving a message where your scent is the strongest. Dogs that are permitted on the bed are more likely to soil the bed. But, of course, understanding all this is of no comfort if your mattress is permanently stained. What is required here is a vigorously pursued housebreaking technique that is implemented until successful, no matter how long it takes. Another solution (as an adjunct to housebreaking, not a substitute) is crating your dog when you leave the house. We'll come to that in a bit.

HOW TO HOUSEBREAK YOUR DOG

Basic Housebreaking

The object of housebreaking is to condition the dog to relieve himself outdoors when being walked. Housebroken dogs will conform to a walking schedule created by you or they will signal you when they have an urgent need to do their business. Your goal must be to have a completely housebroken dog and nothing less. Halfway measures are worse, in a way, than none at all: you can never be sure of what you'll come home to. Usually, a dog that is not housebroken is confined to one small location when the family leaves, and the mess is localized. That, at least, is easier to clean and far less upsetting.

To housebreak a dog you must follow four steps:

1. Restrict the dog's movements.
2. Establish a feeding and walking schedule.
3. Apply consistent praise and correction.
4. Control the dog's scent posting.

None of these steps is complicated or even difficult to remember. Housebreaking is a simple training technique that conditions the dog's mind and body with regard to where and when to relieve himself. Once you have accomplished housebreaking, your dog's mindset will be geared for basic dog obedience. One last word before starting the training . . . linoleum!

The perfect portable gate for confining a dog

Step One

Select a small room or portion of a room where you can restrict the dog's movements. The use of a portable gate that jams against both ends of a doorway can be extremely helpful. When you confine a dog to a small room or area, it is essential that you not close the door, thus isolating the dog from family life. Check with a hardware store or browse through dog equipment catalogs to find a gate. You should have no problem finding a gate, as they are quite common. (Keep the fact in mind, however, that some gates are better than others.) You must be resigned to the fact that the young dog must remain in this confined space all day and all night except when you walk him. The dog may be removed from this area for play and socializing if you have the time to watch him carefully for the signs that indicate he has to "go." These signs include sniffing the ground, squatting, turning in circles, trying to find the door, or general hyperactive behavior. A puppy or young dog will have to "go" immediately after eating or drinking, upon awakening from a nap or deep sleep, after playing, and approximately every two hours of the waking day. A three-month-old puppy can make it through the night without relieving himself as long as he has not been fed, given water, or allowed to run around before bedtime.

When you restrict the dog's activity to one small area, you are taking advantage of his instinctive need to keep his den free of any odor that would reveal his presence to a predator. The smaller the restricted area, the less likely he is to have "accidents." If the dog is in the kitchen or bathroom, lay down several thicknesses of newspaper to facilitate a cleanup. It is vitally important to never let the dog think of the restricted area as a form of punishment. Although he will want to come out as often as he can, you should try, at the very least, to make the confinement area as pleasant as possible. Do your best to allow the dog enough room to walk around a bit. Also, try to pick an area where he can see out to the rest of the house. Feed and water the dog in this area. Give him a nylon chew toy, but don't provide him with balls or play-provoking toys which might trigger the need to eliminate. Taking your dog out to relieve himself is the next step.

Step Two

A word about the food you give the dog. Housebreaking cannot possibly be taught if the dog suffers from diarrhea or has a loose stool. If that is the dog's current condition, have him examined by a veterinarian for worms or other internal parasites. If the dog's bowel movements are fine, avoid introducing stomach upset. Maintain the present diet and do not change it during the housebreaking period, which, under normal circumstances, should not last more than two weeks. A well-balanced canine diet consists of protein, carbohydrates, fats, vitamins, and minerals in the proper proportion as recommended by your vet. Your dog can achieve a proper diet with a premium commercial dog food.

It is now time to consider a feeding and walking schedule that will be adhered to rigidly. Your dog's body will regulate itself to accommodate the schedule. Put nothing in the dog's body unless it is dictated by the schedule. A crucial point: Every time you feed or water the dog he must be taken out for a walk soon afterward so that he can urinate and/or defecate.

The following procedure is correct for *all* dogs, whether they live in apartments or in homes with fenced yards or acreage to run around in. Select a location that is suitable and acceptable for walking your dog. It must be a place that will not upset your neighbors when they see your dog relieve himself. Naturally, you will be prepared with the proper equipment and materials for cleaning up afterward. Scoopers and plastic bags are for sale everywhere and by law must be used in most large cities. When you take the dog out he must be properly leashed at all times, not only for the sake of the law, the dog's safety, and your neighbors' comfort, but for the sake of successful housebreaking. You cannot train a dog that is not under control at all times. Once the dog relieves himself in a specific location, he is going to want to return to that location every time you take him out. He will be drawn to this place by scent and by habit. During the housebreaking period (approximately two weeks) the sole point of the walk should be to allow the dog to eliminate. Do not allow this period to be consumed by sightseeing, play, or exercise. There will be plenty of time for that in the years to come. Take the dog to the "business" area, make sure he relieves himself, and then return home. Some dogs need a longer walk than others before relieving themselves.

The closer you stick to the schedule, the faster you begin to regulate the dog's body to conform with your needs. If your dog is between the ages of three and five months, he will be eating three meals a day. During the housebreaking period, do not leave water down for him at all times or you will delay the success of the training. When you feed the dog, make it a meal to be given at a precise time and allow exactly five minutes to eat. If the dog hasn't eaten by then, remove the dish. Allow him another five minutes for drinking after you serve the water bowl and then remove that, too. If the dog indicates a great thirst between scheduled watering times, give him an ice cube or two to tide him over. The following schedule must be strictly enforced.

FEED-WATER-WALK-RETURN SCHEDULE

Early morning	Walk the dog and return to area
One half-hour later	Feed, water, walk, and return to area
Mid-morning	Water, walk, and return to area
Past noon	Feed, water, walk, and return to area
Mid-afternoon	Water, walk, and return to area
Late afternoon	Water, walk, and return to area
Early evening	Feed, water, walk, and return to area
Before retiring	Walk and return to area for the night

During the day and evening you may remove the puppy from the restricted area for play and attention. Watch carefully for signs that he has to "go." If he does, take him out for a walk. That is the only part of the schedule that you may violate. Do not feed or water the dog at night during housebreaking and do not provide any snacks between meals. How and when to praise the dog is extremely important and is discussed in the next step.

Step Three

Because a dog's instinctive need to live with and be part of a pack is so strong, he thrives on various forms of acceptance and feels dejected by firm criticism. The principle of *praise and correction* is based on this pack instinct. Notice that the word *punishment* does not enter into this principle. Hitting a dog or scolding him too harshly for housebreaking mistakes may get the desired results to some degree, but the price paid in self-confidence and personality is too great. If you want a dog that is terrified of you, then you are reading the wrong book. Fear in a dog builds walls between the animal and his family. Fear can also create shyness and biting behavior. An abused dog sooner or later gets back at the abuser.

When you praise a dog you are instilling in him a desire to do what you want him to do and to work hard for your praise. It is the best form of motivation. The reward is greatly appreciated. If the dog does something properly, don't hold back. Tell him how wonderful he is. Praise is a verbal compliment that should be given with enthusiasm. "Good Girl!" or "Attaboy!" are good examples of effective verbal praise.

A correction, on the other hand, is the exact opposite of praise. If the dog fails to obey or does something wrong, *correct* him. Corrections are a form of rejection. As the exact opposite of praise, corrections teach the dog what not to do. The important word is *teach*. Although corrections are negative in nature, they are not the same as punishment.

The dog feels the correction when a choke collar tightens for an instant around his neck. The trainer has given a quick tug on the leash that is hooked to the choke collar. It is not painful, but it is uncomfortable and somewhat of a surprise. The tug must always be accompanied by a firm "No!" from the trainer. During housebreaking, a noisy shake can is also a useful correction tool. If you take a clean, empty soda can, insert five pennies or other metal objects into it, and tape it closed, you have a terrific noise-maker. By shaking the can vigorously and saying "No!" in a firm tone of voice, you can effectively correct the dog from across the room without the aid of a leash and collar. The effect is to startle the dog and get his immediate attention while delivering the negative message.

Correct the dog during housebreaking when he is in the process of making a mistake. During the puppy's play periods he will no doubt run around the house. If he begins to urinate or defecate you must correct him by shaking the can and saying "No!" in a loud, firm tone of voice. Then immediately scoop him up, grab the leash, attach it, and take him outside to his usual spot. Once there he will probably relieve himself again. When he does, give him heaps upon heaps of praise. You must always do this during the housebreaking period. It takes repetition for the dog to understand what it is that earns him your praise or your rejection. However, if you do not correct the dog *as he is in the process of an "accident"* the correction will hold no meaning for the dog. It will have been a wasted effort.

Do not underestimate the importance of your response to the dog. Praise is the most effective reinforcement of training there is. It is absolutely vital that you lavishly praise your dog every time he relieves himself outdoors in an acceptable location. Every time you walk the dog, be prepared to praise him for doing the correct thing. It is an essential part of training. Avoiding future mistakes is the next step.

Step Four

Just as scent posting works for the trainer during housebreaking, it can also work against her. When the puppy "lets go" on the floor, he has, for all intents and purposes, "marked" the territory. No matter how thoroughly you clean the spot, an odor detected only by the dog will remain. This scent post will always draw the dog back to further mark it. In plain terms, once the dog has peed in one location he is going to do it again and again unless you get rid of that scent. The same thing happens when the dog defecates.

Two things must be accomplished here. First, the scent must be obliterated. Second, remove the stain so the dog cannot see it. Only an odor neutralizer can actually change the scent chemically, as opposed to simply covering the scent with a perfume. Soap and water, ammonia, detergent, and other cleaning products are ineffective. Several commercially prepared odor neutralizers are sold in pharmacies and pet supply stores. The leading neutralizer is called *Nilodor*. It is a highly concentrated liquid that requires no more than a few drops. To remove the visible evidence of a stain on a hard surface is easy. Cold or warm water and detergent will do the trick. Cold water and seltzer are effective for cleaning a washable carpet. If the urine or feces causes a visible stain on a carpet, use a 1:1 solution of cold water and vinegar. Once the spot is cleaned, apply odor neutralizer. Its mint odor usually repels dogs.

Success and Failure

Housebreaking is accomplished within one week for some dogs and within four weeks for others. The average dog catches on in about two weeks if the trainer has rigidly adhered to the regimen. You know your dog is housebroken when he keeps his own area spotless, has almost no "accidents" when allowed to run around the house, and begins to go to the door when he wants to be walked. Then it will be possible to give the dog more freedom and less supervision. It will still be necessary to confine him to his area when you leave the house. Still, you may begin to test him by releasing him from his area as you leave the house for fifteen minutes. Each day increase the length of time he is left alone without restriction.

If the dog should have a housebreaking failure after the training program has been successfully completed, you may choose to repeat the process for one week. Another option is to hook the leash to his collar and walk him to the mess. In a very firm tone of voice say, "No! No! No!" Insist that he look at the mess as you clean it up. Immediately walk him to his outdoor spot, allow him to relieve himself (even if it's only a tinkle), give him great praise, and take him back and pray.

WORKING PARENTS/ SCHOOL-AGE KIDS

It is extremely difficult to housebreak a dog while no one is home. Some will tell you it has been done, and indeed they are probably correct, but it is very difficult. It depends upon the individual dog's physical and emotional needs, as well as the animal's temperament. A hysterical, anxiety-ridden puppy is simply not going to respond to housebreaking when left alone for four, five, or eight hours during the day.

Certain breeds are noted for being difficult to housebreak. Siberian Huskies, Beagles, and the Bichon Frise are examples of breeds that do not thrive when left alone, especially at an early age. No puppy feels good about being alone, to be sure, but some breeds take it harder than others. Dogs express their anxiety as well as their submissiveness through their eliminative activity. One must understand that there can be no guarantee that a puppy left alone during the day can be housebroken properly.

The requirement during housebreaking to schedule a puppy's regimen of food, water, and walking is necessary in all but very rare cases. All that can be suggested for working parents and school-age kids is that they acquire the dog at the beginning of a long holiday period, such as spring break or summer vacation, so that the puppy is not left alone for the first week or two. If it's too late and you already have the dog, pay someone to come to your home during the day to maintain the proper schedule for you. In this situation a wire crate is extremely useful. However, it is very bad for either a puppy or a grown dog to spend its entire day in the confinement of a dog crate. A pup can easily become depressed and fall into bad health. It may even develop a personality disorder. No matter what anyone tells you, a puppy that spends its entire day alone in confinement will never be totally housebroken and will never realize its potential as a happy, joy-giving pet.

Examine the Feed-Water-Walk-Return schedule provided earlier. Note that eight walks a day are recommended. Some breeds (and individual dogs within a breed) are able to adjust to a tighter schedule and still be housebroken. You might be able to eliminate the mid-morning walk along with the mid-afternoon walk if you can persuade a friend, neighbor, or paid individual to come in at noon and feed, water, walk, and return the dog to his crate or area of confinement. In any case, it is absolutely essential that the animal not be left alone with a bowl of food or water. Food and water simply stimulate the digestive reflex and create a need to eliminate.

I suggest you leave on a radio tuned to soothing music or an all-day talk show. Leave the dog chew toys, a favored blanket, or other reassuring objects. These efforts still represent a compromise, albeit one that might work. If none of these suggestions work, someone is going to have to come in and stay with the dog at various times during the day. Unfortunately, there is no other solution, in my opinion.

PAPER-TRAINING

Much difficulty and confusion surround the subject of paper-training. Most training courses and most dog trainers tell us that we must decide whether or not we want our dog to be housebroken or paper-trained. Paper-training means that the dog has been taught *never* to soil anywhere in his home except where newspapers are spread out. Further, the dog may only "go" when he lets you know he needs to "go" or is told to "go." We're also told that trying to teach your dog to use both newspapers indoors and the street outdoors leads to confusion in the dog and ultimate disaster. Confusing the issue even further, those same trainers tell us to spread papers down on the floor in the dog's confinement area during housebreaking. Having done that, it would seem that you are still teaching the dog to use papers and the street.

In truth, some dogs can learn to use newspaper indoors, when necessary, and the street, as well, without dumping on your couch, carpet, or stairway. It is also true, however, that many dogs cannot be paper-trained. So what do you do? If you have a toy breed or even a small- to medium-sized dog, paper-train him. A large male dog, on the other hand, will be more likely to lift his hind leg to urinate and create a new design on your wallpaper. If you are adventuresome, first housebreak the dog and then paper-train him. It may work out. If it does, it's really great. You can use the street in nice weather and paper the dog indoors when it rains, is too late, too cold, or too scary to go out.

When you are housebreaking the dog it is a good idea to spread some newspapers on part of the floor of the dog's confinement area. He is definitely going to eliminate in his area during the early stages of training and the papers help to clean it up. Most dogs hit the papers most of the time. But this fact has nothing whatsoever to do with paper-training. During housebreaking you are simply using some paper for the sake of convenience.

When you paper-train your dog, do everything exactly the same as in the housebreaking technique, with a couple of exceptions. The place you choose in which to restrict the dog should be the place you plan to always use as the dog's newspaper area for eliminating indoors. Instead of walking the dog after each feeding and watering, change the newspapers. On the first day, cover the entire floor of his restricted area with papers. When you change the papers for the first time save one soiled sheet and place it on the spot farthest away from the doorway, under fresh paper. This approach will attract the dog to that spot for his next squirt. Always repeat the same procedure in order to get the dog to eliminate in the same general area. After the first day do not cover the entire floor with paper. Leave one small area of the floor uncovered. On each succeeding day use slightly less paper. Your goal is to have the dog confine his eliminations to the paper only. Watch the dog carefully and use the shaker can accompanied with a firm "No!" if he starts to use the uncovered floor. It can take only five days to complete the training, but count on more than that. The dog is paper-trained when he goes only on paper even though most of the floor is uncovered. Reread the earlier section on housebreaking to better understand what you will need to do for paper-training.

USING A COLLAPSIBLE WIRE CRATE FOR HOUSEBREAKING

For those who are willing to go to the expense, I recommend using a collapsible wire dog crate. A crate is an extremely effective tool for housebreaking and it provides sanctuary for the dog as well. This bit of classic dog equipment appeals to the dog's instinct to live in a den. A dog crate is a rectangular box that is most commonly made out of wire. Crates generally feature a metal or wood floor and they can be purchased in sizes suitable for all dogs. They only *look* like cages with doors. If used properly, they tie in directly with your dog's desire to maintain an inner core territory similar to a doghouse or, if he were in the wild, a den.

When housebreaking your dog with a crate, do everything as outlined in the housebreaking section. However, use the crate as the area of confinement rather than your kitchen or bathroom. This method is better because the dog is not underfoot and he is given a place that will always be his exclusive domain. Once the training is completed, the crate may be used as a doghouse with the wire door open. Most dogs then go in and out of the crate at their own discretion. Puppies accept the crate in a short time as long as they are not forced into it or placed there for punishment. Set it up in an area near family activities, such as the hallway. Be certain it is placed away from sources of direct cold or heat. If you place a few toys and a mat or blanket inside, you will create a friendly sanctuary for the dog. If

you drape an old sheet over the top, the crate becomes more like a doghouse, offering much privacy.

The dog's association with the crate must always be a positive one. Never send a dog to its crate for punishment. Some trainers place a food reward in the back of the crate before confining the dog inside. This action creates a pleasant association for the dog when entering the crate. Except at night, a dog should never be crated for more than three or four hours at a time.

The crate will prove useful in other ways. When traveling with your dog, the crate becomes a portable den providing security, comfort, and safety. Depending upon the size, it can fit into the back seat of a sedan or station wagon. Confined in the crate, your dog cannot stick his head out the car window or distract the driver. A crate is also a valuable place to put your dog during periods of chewing, begging, jumping, and nipping. It can be used as part of an overall obedience training program, or simply as a way of confining the animal and preventing him from getting into trouble. When transporting your dog by airplane, a specially designed travel crate is required. It is made of a highly durable, hardened plastic material that can also be used in the home on a regular basis.

The crate you buy should be long enough to permit your grown dog to stretch out and it should be high enough for him to sit up without hitting his head. Construct a wooden partition for your puppy so that there is just enough room for him to lie down or sit up. The crate should never offer the dog more space than necessary or it will lose its den-like quality. As the puppy grows, increase the space for it by moving the partition back. This equipment is useful, humane, and appreciated by most dogs.

Dogs are our favorite pets because they blend instantly with any family or simply create a family where there was none before. Although they are frequently acquired for children, few adults can resist the unabashed enthusiasm of a dog, whose greatest joy is to be in the company of humans. There isn't a dog alive that cannot find its way into the human heart. Choosing a dog and learning to live with it is a major event and a welcome addition to our lives. The family dog is a four-legged relative who plays a unique role in the human comedy as friend and soulmate, as stimulating playmate and responsive companion. A dog is an endearing friend who always listens and gives the best advice, which is to say, no advice at all. A dog may be one of the few constants in an ever-changing world. It is not difficult to choose the perfect dog for you and your family because there isn't a dog that isn't perfect for someone's family.

INDEX